The Ever-Expansive Spirit of God

This is what the Lord Almighty says:
administer true justice,
show mercy and compassion to one another,
do not oppress the widow or the fatherless,
the alien or the poor.
In your hearts do not think evil of each other.

Zechariah 7:9-10

The Ever-Expansive Spirit of God

For All Who Feel Left Out

Bishop Peggy A. Johnson

The Ever-Expansive Spirit of God
For All Who Feel Left Out
by Peggy A. Johnson

Edited by Gregory F. Augustine Pierce
Designed and typeset by Andrea Reider
Cover Image from Adobe Stock Photos

Copyright © 2023 by Peggy A. Johnson

Scripture verses are from *The Message: Catholic/Ecumenical Edition* © 1993, 1994, 1995, 1996, 2000, 2001, 2002, 2013 by Eugene H. Peterson. Used with permission of Nav Press Publishing Group. All rights reserved.

Quotations by others were considered to be either in the public domain or fair use.

Published by ACTA Publications, Chicago, Illinois, www.actapublications.com, 800-397-2282.

All rights reserved. No part of this publication may be reproduced or transmitted in any form or by any means, electronic or mechanical, including photocopying and recording, or by any information storage and retrieval system, including the Internet, without permission from the publisher. Permission is hereby given to use short excerpts with proper citation in reviews and marketing copy, bulletins and handouts, and scholarly papers.

Library of Congress Control Number: 2023933661
ISBN: 978-0-87946-724-1
Printed in the United States of America by Total Printing Systems
Year 30 29 28 27 26 25 24 23
Printing 10 9 8 7 6 5 4 3 2
Text printed on 30% post-consumer recycled paper.

CONTENTS

Introduction		1
1	"Deaf Drag Queen"	5
2	"He's Now Emily"	12
3	"Precious Alternate Planet"	19
4	"A House Divided"	26
5	"Chargeable Offenses"	35
6	"The Trial"	42
7	"Smoldering Ash"	50
8	"Precious Secret"	57
9	"Pink Tights"	66
10	"Surgery"	75
11	"General Conference 2016"	81
12	"Annual Conferences 2016"	88
13	"Jurisdictional Conference 2016"	93
14	"Gay Pride Parade 2017"	99
15	"Commission for the Way Forward"	104

16	"Town Hall Meetings 2019"	111
17	"In a Relationship"	119
18	"Special Session of General Conference 2019"	126
19	"Aftermath"	135
20	"Tear Down the Wall"	142
21	"The Protocol"	148
22	"COVID-19"	156
23	"Pandemic of Racism"	165
24	"Engagement"	171
25	"Disaffiliations of the Heart"	178
26	"Unmoored"	184
27	"The Reveal"	191

Dedicated to
Rev. Mary Charlotte Johnson,
the love of my life.

INTRODUCTION

> Body and soul, I am marvelously made!
> I worship in adoration—what a creation!
> You know me inside and out,
> you know every bone in my body;
> You know exactly how I was made, bit by bit,
> how I was sculpted from nothing into something.
> Like an open book, you watched me
> grow from conception to birth;
> all the stages of my life were spread out before you,
> The days of my life all prepared
> before I'd even lived one day.
>
> Psalm 139:14-16 *(The Message)*

During my tenure as an episcopal leader, I have struggled mightily with the church's official stance on homosexuality. According to the United Methodist *Book of Discipline*, people who identify as "self-avowed and practicing homosexuals" cannot be ordained as clergy.

THE EVER-EXPANSIVE SPIRIT OF GOD

Furthermore, weddings and holy unions that solemnize gay marriages cannot be conducted by our clergy or be performed in our UMC church buildings. For more than fifty years, our denomination has struggled with this official position as it embodies both theological and social justice concerns.

This book begins with some accounts of my life as a pastor in an all-Deaf congregation in Baltimore, Maryland. I highlight my encounters with the Deaf gay community as well as transgender folks, both in the congregation and in the Annual Conference where I served. I share stories about my election to the episcopacy and the years of my service in the Philadelphia Area of the United Methodist Church.

The controversy around same-gender marriage, sexual orientation, gender identity, and what it means to keep in a covenantal relationship with fellow United Methodists of differing opinions is at the center of this book. I engaged in many other ministries during my tenure as bishop, but I am laser-focused here on this one topic. It is a deeply personal story, full of honest reflections on my journey as a Christian, a minister of the Gospel, and a leader in the church. I am also the wife of a transgender woman and the mother of an adult gay son who is in a committed relationship.

INTRODUCTION

At the time of this writing the United Methodist Church continues to be strongly divided and discussions around separation and disaffiliation are ongoing. Some of our churches have left the denomination already. Yet the ever-expansive Spirit of God continues to draw more diverse people together in love and fellowship.

In 2008, I was elected a bishop of the United Methodist Church at a session of the Northeastern Jurisdictional Conference in Harrisburg, Pennsylvania. I retired as an active bishop on September 1, 2021. On January 1, 2023, I began serving an interim assignment as the bishop of the New England Annual Conference where the debate continues.

It is my hope that people will look back on this era in the life of the United Methodist Church twenty years from now and ask, "What were they thinking?" I hope I will be able to say, "This was simply a part of the journey that brought us to a healthier, more inclusive place."

Some of the names and details in these pages have been changed to protect people's privacy, but I assure you the stories are true. My observations and interpretations may not reflect the perspective of others, but I am indebted to the many friends and colleagues who have supported me on this journey.

THE EVER-EXPANSIVE SPIRIT OF GOD

This book of memories, about how I came to experience and believe, is my gift to the church…and to you, dear reader. We are all, indeed, marvelously made.

> Bishop Peggy A. Johnson, retired
> Carrollton, Virginia
> Feast of the Epiphany, 2023

Note. All royalties from the sale of this book are being donated to Christ United Methodist Church of the Deaf, 1040 S. Beechfield Avenue, Baltimore, Maryland.

1

"DEAF DRAG QUEEN"

"He always loved Halloween," his sister Jean said as she handed me a tattered black and white photograph from a pile of random family snapshots. In the picture was what appeared to be a large woman in a satin, low-cut evening gown. "She" had a five-o'clock shadow, big hands, and on her head was a curly platinum-blond wig.

The person in the photo was Jean's deceased brother, Walter, in costume at some party long ago. Walter had died a few days before, and I was with Jean in his tiny inner city row house in Baltimore, sitting around a kitchen table with a single light bulb hanging from the ceiling. We were preparing for the funeral that would be held at the Deaf Church later that week.

"He liked Halloween, all right," I thought, turning my head so Jean couldn't see me smile.

Walter was one of my earliest memories from the time when I began serving the Christ United Methodist

Church of the Deaf in Baltimore, Maryland, as its pastor in the late 1980s. In the early days of the HIV/AIDS epidemic, the Deaf Community was hard-hit, due to their lack of knowledge about the disease. A local gay organization was hosting a city-wide HIV/AIDS education event, and the Deaf community was invited. One of the Deaf leaders asked me to interpret for the workshop. I declined because I did not feel I had gained enough skill in interpreting and because I was wary of what this conference might involve.

***

Up until that time, I did not know much about the gay community. I still had some theological reservations about homosexuality back then, concerns that I dealt with later as I began to understand the Deaf gay community better and observed how discrimination and rejection had victimized them.

The Scriptural mandates of love and reaching out with compassion to people on the margins of life has always made a lot more sense to me than words about God's judgment and wrath. People were often using the Bible as a weapon to ban me from being a woman in ministry, and I saw first-hand the damnation of gay people in the same way. Yet I knew the few scripture verses in the Bible that seem to point to homosexuality as a sin were written in a much different time and culture.

"DEAF DRAG QUEEN"

I declined the offer to interpret for this HIV/AIDS event mostly because there was going to be a banquet after the workshop at a gay bar, known as the "Hole," in a red-light district of the city. So I turned the job over to another United Methodist pastor who was serving another Deaf congregation at the time. The event at the "Hole" that night included a "Drag Queen Beauty Pageant." According to my clergy friend who interpreted that night, my church member Walter won first prize.

~

Walter had attended my church from time to time, always dressed in bright colors that sometimes matched and sometimes didn't. He loved to bake and often made ornately decorated sheet cakes for the church's pot-luck dinners. At Christmas, he would make the most delicious paper-thin sugar cookies. He also transformed his south Baltimore row house into a Christmas wonderland with old-fashioned colored lights hanging in the windows and a train garden that took up the entire living room—along with life-sized pictures of Santa Claus and the Virgin Mary.

Walter was friendly and kindhearted, gave generously to anyone who needed help, took in strangers and homeless people, and loved Elvis Presley. When it wasn't the Christmas season, Walter's living room was filled with Elvis memorabilia.

THE EVER-EXPANSIVE SPIRIT OF GOD

In later years, Walter became more active at the church. He joined the Deaf choir and signed dramatic songs, with large and expressive gestures. He never missed a Tuesday night choir practice, even though he had to walk three miles because he had no car. Walter was the star of almost all the Bible dramas that were presented during worship because of his natural flair for acting.

While his sister and I were examining the photographs and talking about Walter's funeral, she leaned over, looked me in the eye and said in a whisper, as if someone might be listening, "I think my brother was gay."

I wondered how she could possibly have thought that I didn't know that by now. Before I could respond, she continued, earnestly and wistfully, "It was really all our mother's fault. She wanted a girl and so she always treated him like a daughter. That's how he got that way. He was always different. After he got out of high school he got married, but that didn't work out. Walter was always hanging out with those Deaf guys with the leather jackets."

Those "guys with the leather jackets" were Walter's friends from the gay group known as the "Deaf Leather Club." He was a respected member of that organization who always attended the funerals of the members who died from AIDS and helped with their conferences and events. In his gay circle of friends, he was at home, accepted, influential, and important; he was someone that mattered. He told me once that he won the Drag Queen Beauty Pageant every year, so after a while they stopped having the competition because it was no contest. He held the distinction of being the "Best Deaf Drag Queen Ever."

Jean and I finished planning the funeral. I jotted down everything she said about his life as we sat in that kitchen, but I marveled at how little about Walter his family really knew. Like many Deaf family members, he was an outsider, one they acknowledged with distant politeness, but one they did not really know. No one in the family had learned much sign language, so conversations with him were short and superficial. The little glimpses of his gay life that they did know about was like another world to them.

Sadly, it was the same story at the Deaf church. His cake-making, cleaning, painting, moving furniture, and cooking at the fundraiser dinners were all appreciated, but his homosexuality bothered the more traditionally minded members. "The Bible says that homosexuality is a sin" some would say. A member of the choir made him promise "never to be gay again," and he gave her his word. I can only imagine how that hurt him. The Deaf community sometimes rejected their own who were engaging in controversial activity that might shine a negative light on the community. Thus, the sanctions they levied against their own members were even more punitive and unreasonable at times than what others did to them.

THE EVER-EXPANSIVE SPIRIT OF GOD

Walter's family found his body early one Monday morning in his row house in the living room, next to the big picture of Elvis. He had died of a heart attack, one that was probably brought on by his chronic emphysema and working too hard at church the weekend before. Every choir member, as well as his entire family, came for the wake and/or funeral. Many of his gay friends were there, too, wearing their leather jackets.

We signed his favorite songs, and I preached a sermon about the love God promised to all people. We played *Ain't Nothing but a Hound Dog* (Walter's favorite Elvis Presley song) for the recessional hymn as the casket was carried down the center aisle of the church. Walter's family cooked a generous chicken and ham dinner for everyone, including all the Deaf people in the congregation, which they enjoyed in the basement fellowship hall following the service.

I went upstairs to the sanctuary to turn off the lights and found one of the Deaf choir's members, standing in front of the altar, loudly sobbing. I asked her if she wanted to talk, and she launched into an impassioned tirade about Walter and his homosexuality. After he had promised her that he would "never be gay again" he had not kept his promise. Apparently, rumors continued to spread about his alliances, and she had heard about it.

"Now he is going to hell for this," she exclaimed, with an especially strong sweep of the arm as she signed the word *hell*. "He was a good person in many ways, but he cannot get to heaven because he is gay, and the Bible says that there are no gay people in heaven."

I paused, took a deep breath, and signed, "I don't believe that God sends gay people to hell. I think the grace and love of God is bigger than all of this. God makes all kinds of people, straight and gay. Walter believed in Jesus. That is all that matters."

She shook her head and left the sanctuary, inconsolable, still crying with her Deaf voice, sobs that echoed down the long hallway.

I remained in the sanctuary alone. A few stray flowers from the casket had fallen on the floor, and I wandered down the aisle picking them up. I wondered: *Why did his family have to blame his mother for Walter's homosexuality? He was gay because he was gay; God made him that way! Can't it ever be okay with people that some humans on this planet are gay? Why did the Deaf church have to be yet another place of rejection where Walter was told on a regular basis that he was a sinner and forced to deny who he was in order to get along with people?*

Later I would come to learn a great deal more about the issues of sexual and gender diversity in the context of church life. I thank God for Walter, the "Best Deaf Drag Queen Ever," who taught me much about his world and sealed in my heart the belief that LGBTQIA+ people are children of God, like all people. The church should respect and include them and celebrate their wonderful giftedness as part of the Body of Christ that God intended.

2

"HE'S NOW EMILY"

I had never in my life met a person who was gender dysphoric or transgender. As a child I had known a boy who always played with dolls, but beyond that my young life was binary, divided female and male, pink and blue. I had heard about the famous Christine Jorgensen, who had a sex change operation years ago, but I had never known anyone personally who believed they were living in the wrong body. All that changed one day, when, as a pastor serving in Baltimore, I received a call from a colleague in ministry who said, "You know Roger Evans, right?"

"Yes," I replied, recalling our clergy colleague.

"Well, Roger is now Emily! He had a sex change operation and left his church," my friend said, and together we shared our genuine shock and disbelief. I could not imagine what Roger/Emily could have been thinking. He was a regular-looking guy whom I had known for several years. He was married and had two children. It did not make any sense to me that he would want to become a woman. This was in 2004.

Among the clergy back then, there was much conversation about this person's status as a pastor. Was Roger still the same person as Emily? Wasn't he/she still ordained? Ordained elders in the United Methodist Church are guaranteed a position with full compensation, so some wondered, "How would churches accept a pastor who had gender re-assignment surgery?" and "Is he/she still eligible to be a pastor if no church will accept him/her?"

There were more questions than answers. These were obviously difficult conversations for Emily, and the negative response from some clergy was strong. She took a leave of absence at the time.

I had the opportunity to talk with Emily some time after her transition. Employed at a restaurant near the Deaf church, she was instrumental in hiring a Deaf woman for a part-time job there. Emily explained to me that all her life she had felt she was female, and that this surgery and life transition were crucial in allowing her to finally have peace. To a degree she was very much a woman, but I could still see Roger in there somehow. I felt a deep compassion for Emily as this decision had cost her a great deal. Although she had been a highly effective pastor, she now worked in a much lower-paying, secular job. She found hospitality and support from one of the United Methodist Churches in the area, but many rejected and criticized her. Eventually she went on to serve as a pastor of other congregations, including a United Methodist Church in Florida in her retirement.

About three years later, another pastor, this time a female, transitioned to male. This created the predictable "firestorm" among some clergy. But since no rules existed forbidding transgender ministers in the United Methodist *Book of Discipline*, and since there was a welcoming congregation willing to accept him as their pastor, this pastor's transition was no more than a name change in the Annual Conference journal. She continued to serve that congregation for several more years and eventually moved on to do other kinds of work.

The following year, in 2008, I attended the United Methodist General Conference in Ft. Worth, Texas, as an elected delegate and was assigned to the "Faith and Order" legislative committee. In committees, the delegates discuss every submitted petition and decide which issues to vote on in the larger plenary session, which to combine with other similar questions, and which to discard. All decisions approved at every General Conference later appear in our *Book of Discipline* as our church law. This book is the one we Methodists live by as a denomination, and it is revised every four years.

Due in part to the notoriety of the two transgender pastors in the Baltimore-Washington Annual Conference, the Faith and Order committee that year needed to process several petitions calling for the church to ban transgender people from becoming ordained, like the prohibition we already had on gay clergy. One proposed petition stated, "whatever gender a person has at birth is the one they have to keep in order to be ordained." Essentially, the petition asked candidates for ordained ministry to present their birth certificates as part of the screening process. People who transitioned would not be eligible for ordination if this passed.

To me, the solution did not appear so obvious any more after knowing two clergy colleagues who had transitioned. The problem was not their gender change, I concluded. It was the negative attitude of people who did not understand. I was pleased that our legislative committee chose *not* to bring anti-transgender petitions to the floor of the General Conference that year. There is nothing to this day in the *Book of Discipline* that mentions transgender pastors. What a curious providence that I was a part of that legislative committee in 2008.

God has continuously dropped breadcrumbs of transgender experiences in the pathway of my life. For example, back in the early 2000s I knew a Deaf-Blind man who transitioned to female. I had related to him as Gilbert. For several years we worked together at the annual Deaf-Blind camp sponsored by the Deaf Church I was serving. Gilbert lived on the west coast but would come to the camp and teach Bible Studies, enhanced by his larger-than-life gregarious personality. Then, after camp one year, a letter arrived. Gilbert announced that he was a woman and had changed his legal name to Grace.

Grace wrote to all of us from the Deaf-Blind camp requesting that we send her some size 2X women's clothing to begin her new life as a female. People in the Deaf community, those at camp, and other church people that knew Gilbert had a difficult time accepting this news. Not many people sent clothing or support, but I did, and I kept in contact with her.

Long letters continued to reach me from Grace explaining her failed attempts to find a surgeon who would perform gender-affirming surgery since Medicaid, her only health insurance, did not cover this kind of thing at the time. Grace finally gave up on the idea of surgery and decided just to live as a woman using hormone therapy. She reunited with her former wife, Debbie, who was hard-of-hearing and had some vision loss. The couple lived in subsidized housing for people with disabilities in San Jose, California.

The United Methodist Church sponsored a large international Deaf conference, the first of its kind ever, in

2005. My Deaf congregation served as the host church, and visitors converged on Baltimore from eight international countries. Scholarship money from the mission board was made available for Grace and Debbie to attend this event.

On a bright July day, the pair flew from California to Dulles airport in Virginia. A pastor who lived near the airport picked them up, while I welcomed a large group of Korean guests arriving at the Baltimore airport at the same time. The volunteer pastor at the airport called on his cell phone as he drove Grace and Debbie to Baltimore. "These are some truly interesting people," he said and laughed as he hung up the phone. I wondered what I would see when they arrived.

About an hour later, I got a full view as the two made a grand entrance into the hotel lobby, dressed in matching full-length, taffeta evening gowns and sparkling costume jewelry. Grace had long, strawberry-blond hair. Debbie, whom I had never met, was a petite woman with dark hair and intense brown eyes. The ten-inch difference in height between them added to the strange effect as they stood side by side in their formal attire. The typical dress for this event was summer-time casual. As they approached the conference registration desk, the Deaf Korean visitors stopped what they were doing and stared at them. I suppose they wondered greatly about the customs of Deaf Americans.

The conference went on as planned, with the unusual guests from California seated in the front row, dressed in different evening gowns each day. They explained that they had purchased these clothes from a thrift store after prom season at a very reduced cost. Some Deaf people who knew Grace when she was Gilbert complained to me about the couple's lifestyle, which they assumed was lesbian. For me, it was not hard to accept that Gilbert was now Grace. She seemed so very happy. Who was I to judge a person's inner self? I would later have many more journeys into the world of transgender people.

3

"PRECIOUS ALTERNATE PLANET"

On July 17, 2008, my life and career as a United Methodist minister underwent a dramatic change. I was elected bishop of the denomination on the 9th ballot at the Northeastern Jurisdictional Conference held in Harrisburg, Pennsylvania. The election meant the end of my twenty years of ministry with an amazing Deaf congregation, where I had met people who taught me what it means to hear with the heart and engage in fully inclusive ministry. I had felt for at least three years prior to the election that my days with the Deaf world were ending, and something kept telling me it was time to move on.

When I put my name up as a candidate for election to the episcopacy, it was a definite response to a calling from God, but it felt preposterous. Common sense would say that it was highly unlikely for the likes of me, with my lack of high-level administrative experience, to be elected to this office. However, God continued to drop sufficient hints in my path to make it impossible for me to refuse to run. I joined the election process out of sheer obedience to a tenacious and most unusual call from God

~

Weeks leading up to the meeting in Harrisburg, I found myself in the Deaf church going through all the books and albums, making sure they were in good order. I organized the files, as well as the Bible drama costumes. I visited the Deaf inmates at the state prison and the Deaf patients at the state mental hospital. I had a crazy premonition that I was going to be elected.

The moment the 9th ballot was read, I knew life would never be the same. I became one of the sixty-three residential bishops in the denomination, assigned to work as the spiritual and administrative leader of eight hundred and fifty churches and one hundred thousand United Methodists in the eastern part of Pennsylvania, the state of Delaware, and the Eastern Shore of Maryland in two Annual Conferences (Eastern Pennsylvania and Peninsula-Delaware). Duties included assigning pastors to their churches, solving conflicts and legal issues, presiding over official meetings, keeping the unity of the church, casting the vision for the proclamation of the Gospel, and engaging the church in the work of social justice and mission. In addition, I was to partner with ecumenical and

"PRECIOUS ALTERNATE PLANET"

interreligious communities and serve on agencies and committees of the denomination.

I promised that I would uphold the *Book of Discipline* of the United Methodist Church. This was the book that said that people who are homosexual could not be ordained, that the practice of homosexuality was "contrary to Christian teaching," and forbade clergy from conducting marriages or holy union ceremonies for people who were gay or lesbian. I promised, but I also prayed I would never have to face a painful church trial over these issues.

Twenty years of serving in a Deaf congregation did not exactly qualify me to lead such a large segment of our denomination, but it was my belief that God, "equips the called," not "calls the equipped," and that kept me going. I also knew that my experience working with people on the margins of life was a unique gift. The response of the Deaf church people to my election was one of amazement, shock, and grief. Even though we had talked about it for weeks before the election, my departure was unsettling and puzzling for many, and for me as well.

A busload of Deaf people traveled from Baltimore to Harrisburg for the Episcopal Consecration service on July 18, 2008, at the Grace United Methodist Church. I was the only bishop being consecrated that year in the Northeast Jurisdiction. In attendance were many United Methodist bishops, the delegates to the conference, and

THE EVER-EXPANSIVE SPIRIT OF GOD

an interesting mix of Deaf and Deaf-Blind people, several of whom were using wheelchairs, walkers, and canes. The Deaf choir signed an anthem with the pounding of a bass drum. There were many tears, an abundance of pink flowers in every window, and all the Deaf folks wearing pink scarves. Pink is my favorite color, and it is my name sign in American Sign Language. There was a feeling of incredible honor, as well as unspeakable sadness in the room that day.

Bishop Susan Morrison preached the consecration sermon, and I presided over the Holy Communion celebration with Bishop Joseph Yeakel. After the service, one Deaf woman from the church signed to me, "Let me get this straight. You are now a bishop! Can you still be the pastor of the Deaf church?" I had to tell her that I could never again be their pastor, but I would always keep their culture and beautiful language of signs as a part of my ministry.

Despite the enormous change I was experiencing, I knew that I would forever see things in the light of the culturally Deaf perspective and their tenacious struggle for life and access to communication with the world around them. They live on an alternate planet of sorts, and while I was with them, I received a glimpse of it and felt its sunshine on my face. Their world was sometimes a source of frustration and sometimes even of amusement, but always I appreciated their spirit of resourcefulness and tenacity. Their language of signs fascinated me as

"PRECIOUS ALTERNATE PLANET"

it was expressive in ways in which spoken English falls short.

Texting was a huge vehicle for transmitting Deaf community news. With the touch of a finger anything that was typed into a pager could be forwarded to a vast number of Deaf peoples' text pagers, creating an omniscient loop of communication. (The only part that bothered me was watching the community text one another and drive at the same time!) They also made good use of video phone technology and connected with friends all over the world through the internet.

American Sign Language linguistic expressions are decisive and meaningful. If something was a lost cause they would sign, "NOT WORTH" with a huge sweeping motion of the arms. When something was finally over, the sign for that was an emphatic flick of both wrists, "FINISH." If something was undeniably factual it would be signed, "TRUE WORK." If you missed a part of a conversation and asked to be cut into it you would be told (partly in jest but sometimes not), "TRAIN GONE FINISH" (which meant the topic had been discussed and it is too late to be included).

In American Sign Language grammar, a proper noun is usually signed first, and an adjective would come second. It makes visual sense, but it was amusing to my hearing-world's eye. Burger King Restaurant was, "KING BURGER." A Sloppy Joe sandwich was, "JOE SLOPPY." Radio Shack electronic store was, "SHACK RADIO." Dairy Queen ice cream was, "QUEEN DAIRY."

THE EVER-EXPANSIVE SPIRIT OF GOD

When I was working with Deaf people, I heard with my eyes, I felt with my heart, I talked with my hands, and I never needed to hear at all except when I heard them laughing or crying. Those unique sounds held an insider's warmth for me. They lived on a precious alternate planet that I was privileged to share.

After I officially began my service as a bishop on September 1, 2008, I moved into a huge five-bedroom, six-bathroom house in Phoenixville, Pennsylvania. I was given an administrative assistant, an assistant to the bishop, two offices, a staff of fifty people, and a new computer and cell phone. I received an $80,000 pay raise and went from working with people on the margins of life to ministering to people in the mainstream of life. This new position also felt like an alternate planet. I prayed that the lessons I had learned in working in the Deaf world would always remain a part of me: a concern for the poor, a heart for people with disabilities, a passion for social justice, a sense of humor, a passion for communication, and a humble spirit.

I had learned about the gay, lesbian, and transgender communities from my Deaf congregation, and could see that they were also a marginalized group who suffered much discrimination, even in the Deaf community. It was my prayer that in my role as a bishop I could raise awareness and compassion for them as well. Perhaps the many obstacles that my Deaf congregation and I had faced were preparing me for this new role. I knew in my heart that I was called for such a time as this. And when conversations during a cabinet meeting ran on too long, I knew I could always say "Finish" and take a trip to "King Burger" for a snack.

4

"A HOUSE DIVIDED"

In addition to a consecration service at the time of their election, all recently assigned bishops have an installation ceremony locally. This special worship service and reception provides an opportunity for people to formally greet their new bishop. My installation was held on September 13, 2008, at the Aldersgate United Methodist Church in Wilmington, Delaware. A respectable number of pastors and lay people from both the Eastern Pennsylvania and the Peninsula-Delaware Annual Conferences attended this event.

Many Deaf people from Baltimore came as well; they participated in the service by performing a Bible drama that went along with my sermon text. I chose Matthew 25:31-46, the parable of the final judgement where the sheep and the goats are separated.

I received several gifts that symbolized the various duties of a bishop. Gowned in light blue robes, a choir

"A HOUSE DIVIDED"

from the Delaware Korean UMC sang a magnificent anthem. A representative from the Native American community played a prelude on her indigenous wooden flute. I preached about our mandate from Jesus to minister to the poor, using many personal illustrations. We sang the triumphal closing hymn, Lead on, O King Eternal, and with that, I was duly installed.

At the reception that followed, there was a long receiving line of people I would now be serving, and it was my chance to get to meet some of them one-on-one. Most of the people in line gave me a handshake and a word of welcome, but two encounters proved symbolic in setting the stage for the next chapter in my life. One was an older man who challenged my sermon: "Don't you believe in preaching God's Word?" he demanded, with a spark of fire in his eyes. I assured him I did believe in the Bible.

"You preached about social justice and not about salvation. People are saved by faith in Christ, not by feeding the hungry!" he said. He must have missed that I did mention salvation at the beginning of the sermon. However, the main thrust of my message was about ministry with people living on the margins of life, and I was not going to apologize for it.

The issue of social justice was close to my heart, and in their inaugural sermon bishops are supposed to cast a vision for their leadership. Faith in Christ and works of mercy are not mutually exclusive, but often people lean toward one side or the other in their journey of faith. Clearly this gentleman would have preferred a salvation message, and for him "God's Word" meant that and only that.

In the line standing just behind this gentleman were two women who introduced themselves as a lesbian couple. They smiled and shook my hand vigorously and said they were hoping that my concern for social justice would include them. They reminded me about the *Book of Discipline*'s discriminatory paragraphs.

How sad to be faithful members of a church that denied their humanity and judged them as "contrary to Christian teaching." I have never been sure what "Christian teaching" was in the first place, but some passages in the Bible, if taken literally, say judgmental things about homosexual people. These include passages from Leviticus 20:13 (abomination), Genesis 19:5, 24-25 (God's destruction of a city that engaged in same sex behaviors), Romans 1:26-27 (the Apostle Paul's condemnation of same gender sexual relations) and I Corinthians 6:9-10 (the Apostle Paul's laundry list of behaviors that will bar one from entering heaven). Biblical scholars have debated long and hard about the interpretation of these texts, which have numerous language and cultural interpretations.

The divide between the theologically conservative and liberal sides of the house was set in place long before I became a bishop. Now it was my turn to lead in a way and attempt to hold the two together during a time when homosexuality was becoming increasingly accepted by our society. When I was installed on that sunny day in September, one of the symbolic gifts I received was a clergy stole, symbolizing that I was yoked with Christ to serve the church, the whole church. I did it side by side with the help of the Christ.

As a new bishop, I made rounds to all the groups and committees within the area to get to know the people and their concerns. For the most part, pastors and congregants were gracious and hospitable. I visited every district in both conferences and had listening sessions with groups of all kinds: urban, rural, by the ocean, in the suburbs, in the mountains; there were even three churches on a single island in the Chesapeake Bay. My morning meetings with the clergy were full of questions about my theology and plans for making pastoral appointments.

The evening meetings with the laity included concerns about apportionments (mission dollars that churches are required to pay) and clergy compensation. Gracious receptions followed each meeting, and people lingering for small talk. I also met with committees, caucus groups, presidents of seminaries, directors of camps and conferences, ecumenical partners, and affiliated institutions such as retirement communities and supportive housing programs. Those early months of the honeymoon were a whirlwind of activity, and everyone was gracious.

I received this affirming note after one such meeting:

Dear Bishop Johnson,

When I attended your district meeting the other night, I expected a bishop with a commanding presence and grand sweeping statements. Instead, I beheld a meek, witty woman with a simply profound faith, and I thought: *Wow, this could be fantastic for the UMC around here.* I praise God for giving you the unique gifts he has, and I thank you and honor you.

Early in my tenure I also had a meeting with the theologically conservative group known as the "Evangelical Connection" of the Eastern Pennsylvania Conference. They stood firmly behind the Disciplinary statements that opposed the ordination of gay and lesbian people and same gender weddings. During this conversation, I shared my belief that gay people were not sinners choosing an evil lifestyle, but rather that some people were created by God with a homosexual orientation and that it was one of the many diversities in creation. I promised to uphold the *Book of Discipline*, but I believed that someday these paragraphs denouncing homosexuality and same-gender weddings would be eliminated.

When asked about the scriptures that condemned homosexual behavior, I responded that I had been told in the past that I had no right to be an ordained woman in ministry because of various verses in the Bible. On my first day as a bishop, there was a letter on my desk that

"A HOUSE DIVIDED"

included passages from the letters of the Apostle Paul in the New Testament stating that women should be silent (I Corinthians 14:34) and should not have authority over men (I Timothy 2:12). The anonymous writer called for my immediate resignation.

I reminded the folks at the meeting that in today's United Methodist Church women *can* be ordained (despite Scripture passages seemingly to the contrary), but that prior to 1956 they could not be ordained. That argument did not seem to sway the participants in any way whatsoever on the issue of homosexuality. To my surprise, even the women clergy in the room that night insisted that it was "a different issue altogether."

I asked them to consider the Scriptures and disciplinary paragraphs that support the dignity and worth of all people. Their response was polite but emphatic that they did not agree with me. They cautioned that if the United Methodist Church ever ordained gay and lesbian people or performed gay weddings, donations would be withheld and many people would also leave the church entirely.

As I was leaving the room, a young man, one of the newer pastors at this meeting, followed me out into the hall and whispered, "I agree with you about what you said, but I can't say it in that room." I thought, *How sad for him* and imagined there were many like this young person who were having second thoughts about their long-held conservative beliefs. But speaking out on behalf of homosexual people was personally risky.

I also visited with the "Reconciling Ministry Network" committee of the Eastern Pennsylvania Conference, the theological polar-opposite of the Evangelical Connection. Their goal was to unify people around the issue of full inclusion of the LGBTQIA (Lesbian, Gay, Bi-sexual, Transgender, Queer, Intersex, and A-gender) community into the life of the denomination.

I expected this gathering would be a pleasant experience, given my progressive leanings. What a surprise! They wanted me to promise that I would ordain gay and lesbian candidates for ministry despite the mandates of our denomination's *Book of Discipline*. They were disappointed when I said that I would not break the church laws.

I explained that I wanted full inclusion, but I also had promised to follow the *Book of Discipline*. "We needed to work to change through the normal channels of due process at General Conference and remain faithful to our ministry in the meantime," I said. I suppose I appeared to them as one more self-serving bureaucrat siding with the status quo.

Understandably, people on the progressive side were tired of hearing calls for changing the *Book of Discipline* through our legislative process. Many valiant efforts had gone into proposals to change the church's position on these issues during past sessions of General Conference.

"A HOUSE DIVIDED"

Despite many such attempts, the *Book of Discipline* never changed that much. In fact, it became increasingly more restrictive and punitive as the years went by.

In 1972, the statement about the practice of homosexuality being "incompatible with Christian teaching" first appeared. In later General Conferences, more paragraphs were added. These included: funding restrictions, the prohibition on homosexual clergy ordination, and the prohibition against performing same-gender unions or weddings. Probably the worst addition was the one that stated that being a "self-avowed and practicing" homosexual minister or performing a same-gender unions became a "chargeable offense." That meant a person could go to trial for this. The legislative process was consistently conservative.

The Reconciling Ministry Network committee reminded me that people, especially young people, would be leaving the denomination and we would lose donations if we kept this homophobic position. Both sides were threatening financial and membership loss if I did not follow their way of thinking. Both clearly disliked the other side, and they have had a long and painful history together.

It did not take long for me to realize we were a house divided over many other social issues as well, despite some of our denominations long-held social justice positions. In my conferences, there were sharp lines of controversy around issues such as racism, gun control, the death penalty, gambling, abortion, universal health care, and immigration reform. I prayed earnestly for the wisdom to serve both sides of the house.

5

"CHARGEABLE OFFENSES"

One of the duties of a bishop is to receive and care for formal complaints that are lodged against pastors, as well as lay people, for behaviors known as "chargeable offenses." The *Book of Discipline* provides a list of categories of such actions, and there are guidelines for how to process these charges. Everything must be done with fairness and a careful paper trail of documentation. The goal of every complaint is to solve the matter with what is called a "Just Resolution," which means finding a solution that both parties can accept.

Early in my tenure as bishop, I received a complaint against a pastor who had an extra marital affair. I stumbled through the proceedings, learning my way as I went along. I was constantly calling retired bishops and the conference chancellor for advice. Eventually there was a resolution, but I would soon discover that dealing with chargeable offenses was to become a regular part of my work as a bishop.

***

In the years that followed, there were cases of clergy adultery, child molestation, pornography, indecent exposure, embezzlement, alcoholism, drunk driving, drug addiction, incest, sexual harassment, and sexting. I handled over seventy cases during my tenure as an active bishop. Each one had its own unique set of circumstances and outcomes. In some cases, pastors gave up their ministerial credentials, some took a leave of absence and entered a treatment program or counseling, some went to prison, and one sadly committed suicide. With laypeople, the cases were much fewer and the outcomes were unique in each case.

Much time-consuming investigation had to be done in each case, and sometimes it was hard to know the truth. A pastor's livelihood, family, and career were often on the line. It was vitally important to be fair and merciful to all the parties involved. These were the hardest tasks I ever had to do as a bishop, and sometimes there were no good answers at the end of the day.

***

The hands-down most bone-chilling case, started innocently enough with a call from a man who said he was convinced that his wife was having an affair with the pastor. (I am using all made-up names as I describe this case.) The man's wife, Karen, was the secretary to Pastor Bob at a small country church. The husband, Stan, was to meet me at my office on Thursday of the following week and faxed a signed complaint statement. We would discuss the details in person. When Thursday morning came, Stan did not show up. Instead, the local news service reported that Stan was found dead with a bullet wound to the head and his body was laying on the pastor's desk at the church. The investigators determined that this was a case of suicide, but some of Stan's family members were convinced this was not the case.

Three months before this horror, Pastor Bob's wife, Fran, had been killed in a car accident. According to Pastor Bob, he was driving his wife to the hospital because she complained of a severe headache. On the way to the hospital, a deer ran into the car and Fran was killed from a head injury when the car veered off the road and hit a tree. There was not much of an investigation around this accident, and Pastor Bob received much sympathy from his colleagues and church members. It was doubly sad because his first wife had died twenty years before from an accidental fall and now he had lost second spouse in another tragic way.

Ronda, the suicide victim's sister, continued to contact the District Attorney about her brother's death, claiming that Stan's death was not a suicide. She felt there was foul play involved since word was getting around that Pastor

Bob and Stan's wife were often seen together after Stan's death. Eventually, the DA went to the pastor's house to do an investigation and discovered dried blood on the garage floor. DNA testing proved that it was Fran's blood. One thing led to another and eventually the pastor was on trial for her murder and a staged car accident.

I met with Pastor Bob in my office, and he withdrew his credentials as a Local Pastor in the United Methodist Church so there would be no need for a complaint process. He was later found guilty of Fran's murder and began serving a long prison sentence.

Over a year later, people began to wonder about Pastor Bob's first wife, Marcie, who had died from a head trauma in the basement of the parsonage at a different church twenty years earlier. A new investigation determined that the X-rays taken at that time proved that her slipping and falling down the basement steps could not have produced the extensive head trauma that brought her to the hospital on the night she died.

Many months and court proceedings later, Bob pleaded "no contest" to this murder and waived another trial. This surrealistic story became a topic on CBS's *60 Minutes* and NBC's *Dateline* that year.

Many of the complaints I had to handle were heart-wrenching, but this next story was something all Methodist bishops had to handle. Prior to my tenure as bishop,

"CHARGEABLE OFFENSES"

there was a highly publicized case of a clergy member of the Eastern Pennsylvania Conference who declared openly from the pulpit that she was a lesbian living in a committed relationship. To be such and to openly declare the same was a chargeable offense according to the *Book of Discipline*, and a formal complaint was filed.

This eventually led to a church trial, and the pastor was found guilty and defrocked; but she was later reinstated by a jurisdictional appeal committee and then defrocked again by a ruling of the Judicial Council. This prolonged church legal procedure went on for two years.

Although the pastor had lost her ministerial credentials, the church where she served continued her employment as a lay person, with the same role and compensation. Later she left to pursue a doctoral degree and other work. This brave woman remains to this day a symbol of the movement for equal rights in ministry for people of the LGBTQIA community.

It is my considered opinion that the prohibition against the ordination of gay and lesbian people and/or the performing same-gender weddings in the United Methodist Church should not be lumped into the list of chargeable offenses. Just knowing and announcing oneself to be gay or performing a wedding for one's congregants who are gay should not be an ecclesiastical crime on a list that includes truly egregious misconduct (such as the murder of two wives).

The first case I handled that came close to going to trial involved a pastor having an affair outside of marriage in 2011. We were not able to attain a just resolution, so I turned the case over to the church's Committee on Investigations for further vetting. This committee consisted of elected pastors and lay people chosen to examine a case carefully to determine whether it should or should not go to trial based on the facts.

The committee determined that there was sufficient evidence for a trial. At that point, the pastor withdrew from ministerial office voluntarily. I had no idea how lucky I was when that happened. I was later to learn the great value of having the Committee on Investigations. The 2012 session of General Conference removed it from the *Book of Discipline* altogether. There was no longer a process that afforded a bishop like me more wisdom and scrutiny. The very existence of a Committee of Investigation was removed because it prolonged the trial process (and, I believe, sometimes appeared to serve progressive agendas).

Pastors are under a great deal of personal stress in the ministry. Serving a congregation is not merely preaching on Sunday, visiting the sick, and conducting weddings and funerals. The burden of the pastoral needs of parishioners

"CHARGEABLE OFFENSES"

is often huge, the pay is usually low, and attending to the basic human needs of the surrounding community is simply a necessary part of the work of helping to build the Kingdom of God "on Earth as it is in Heaven." In tough economic times, the church is under even more pressure to be the place of help for many of the woes of the world.

So this stress causes many good people to make bad decisions—clergy and laity alike. Additionally, some not-so-healthy people enter ordained ministry and act out their pathologies on their congregations with a cloak of holiness that the title affords them. Much heartache and trauma can result in cases like these.

The saddest example of this was an anonymous letter I received from a man who is now living in another state. He was a teenage victim of clergy sexual abuse who wanted me to tell the district superintendents (who directly supervise the pastors in the conference) to protect young people like himself. I shared his message with the superintendents, and we sat in silence for a long time.

6

"THE TRIAL"

One Sunday in the fall of 2011, I visited Rev. Frank Schaefer's church near Lebanon, Pennsylvania. The congregation was alive with activity, multi-generational energy, and excellent music. There were two services, an early one that was more traditional in style and a later service that was less formal, with a praise band known as The Damascus Road. Rev. Schaefer was a part of this singing group. Their music was contemporary Christian rock music of a very high quality, and after each song the parishioners literally screamed as if they were attending an outdoor rock concert. The pastor explained to me that the later service was for people who were faith seekers, and the earlier service was for the long-time members.

I preached at both services and left there feeling this was a new model for the church. Nothing that day would have given me even the slightest clue of the storm that was to come.

"THE TRIAL"

A year later, I received a formal, signed complaint against Rev. Schaefer from a member of the church. In the letter, the complainant included a copy of a marriage license from the state of Massachusetts with the pastor's signature. Gay weddings were legal in that state back then, however performing a gay marriage is one of the chargeable offenses in the Methodist Church.

It turned out that several years previously, Rev. Schaefer had been the officiant for his gay son's marriage. It was as an act of love and support on his part. The statute of limitations for filing such a complaint was only weeks before expiration, but suddenly one showed up in this case.

I would have loved to have dodged this issue, but the complaint was technically valid, so it was my duty to proceed with the process as outlined in our church law book. Finding a just resolution between these two parties did not go well, despite several attempts to make peace. Since the 2012 General Conference had voted to discontinue the Committee on Investigations, that helpful resource was gone. Because we could not come to a resolution, therefore, the matter had to go straight to trial. (Much later the Committee on Investigations was reinstated in our *Book of Discipline* as our Judicial Council ruled that eliminating it was unconstitutional, but it was too late for this case).

THE EVER-EXPANSIVE SPIRIT OF GOD

So I sent Rev. Schaefer to trial, and this matter would be decided by a jury of his peers. I wish I would have tried harder, or hired an outside mediator, but I thought at the time I had no other choice. Promising to uphold the *Book of Discipline* and believing that same-gender weddings were acceptable in the eyes of God was a moral dilemma for me. The entire process was fraught with difficulties, delays, and demonization.

For the next six months, my staff and I prepared for the trial. A retired bishop was found to serve as the trial judge. (I had asked nine other bishops before I found one who would agree to do it.) Quite a few lawyers were giving legal advice, there was a clergy counsel for both Rev. Schaefer and the complainant, a jury was carefully selected, and a location for the trial was secured. It was all a terrible, highly publicized drama, and it felt like death by a thousand pin pricks. My faithful and non-judgmental staff was stressed to the brink of exhaustion.

To make matters worse, about a week before the trial some of the ministers in the Eastern Pennsylvania Conference participated in a show of support for the pastor on trial by conducting a same-gender wedding of two gay men at one of our center city Philadelphia churches. The pastor of that church presided at the wedding, and no less than thirty-two clergy (mostly but not all United Methodists), dressed in clerical robes and stoles, participating in a joyous, rainbow colorful event.

News services all over the country had been notified and present. These pastors were breaking the vows of their ordination and the church where the ceremony took place was out of compliance because the *Book of Discipline* forbids gay weddings to be performed on our church premises.

I had met with the lead pastor of the church who then led this mass wedding the following week, and he said he had to do it because it was part of his duty as a pastor to care for his gay parishioners. My heart agreed with him, but clearly what he was going to do was a chargeable offense done to demonstrate the impossibility of stopping this justice movement. There were many progressive pastors in our Annual Conference. All of them who came to that wedding were willing to be charged for what they believed.

The conservative side of the Conference was deeply distressed by this flagrant disobedience to our law book. They complained that pastors had vowed to uphold the church's position at their ordination and were being unfaithful. The progressive pastors seemed pleased with the firestorm they were creating.

There were also people who didn't care one way or the other about what happened at Rev. Schaefer's trial. They were the live-and-let-live centrists. They wanted it all to go away so we could get back to normal, as if there was ever a time when things were what they called "normal." The centrists simply preferred not to take sides.

I took no action against the mass wedding folks. It wasn't in my heart to engage in one more dispute, as the Schaefer trial was challenging enough. I knew that eventually someone would file a complaint, but surprisingly, despite much rumbling, no one came forward at that time.

As we were preparing for the day of the Schaefer trial, I was the object of much public shaming by progressive activists. I received over 400 letters and emails decrying my decision to send Rev. Schaefer to trial. I was called: "Satan," "Pontius Pilate," "Judas," a "Nazi death-camp officer," and a "self-righteous ass hole." I answered each signed letter with respect, and sometimes my reply would create an even more vicious response; sometimes the writer was amazed that I would reply and backed down a bit on their venom, and a few even engaged in civil conversation with me.

One of the most painful attacks came from a seminary student who launched a continuous social media campaign against me. Other social media outlets would pick up his posts with an unflattering picture of my face. One pastor of a large progressive congregation posted continuous critical comments on Facebook that resulted in another batch of unhappy letters on my desk.

I knew that this was the cost of leadership, but it was a dismal, acrid experience. All the while, the conservative folks were sending me letters decrying my lack of action against the pastors who performed the gay wedding in Philadelphia. Their outcry was somewhat more measured and respectful, but some suggested that I needed to resign as bishop.

The church trial was held November 18-19, 2013, and the only role I had in the process was to offer the opening prayer on the front steps of the building. It was held at a gymnasium at one of our conference camps, Camp Innabah, in Spring City, Pennsylvania. Many reporters from the secular and the religious press were there to cover the event. Numerous supporters of Rev. Schaefer were present, clad in rainbow stoles and holding signs and sometimes breaking into songs like *Jesus Loves Me* and *We Shall Overcome* as they stood outside.

It was extremely painful for me to stand on the steps of the gymnasium and look out and see pastors I knew from my home conference who had been at my consecration as a bishop and were now standing there in strong opposition to this trial… and to me. It was equally grievous to see that the pastors from Eastern Pennsylvania were so strongly divided among themselves. Conservative pastors as well as the rainbow-stole contingent were both on hand, and their mutual disrespect for one another hung in the air like a dark cloud before a thunderstorm.

THE EVER-EXPANSIVE SPIRIT OF GOD

An enormous amount of work and effort had gone into preparing for this two-day trial. The goal was to make it as professional and pastoral as possible. There were prayer stations and Holy Communion services and spiritual directors available. The details of providing stenographers, seating arrangements, housing needs, food, and legal counsel were dutifully cared for by the hard-working staff in the conference office. In addition, we gave Rev. Schaefer several weeks of paid renewal leave and cared for his church in his absence. But no amount of preparation and care could take away the pain and sadness of it all.

─────

At the end of the trial, the pastor was found guilty of performing a gay wedding. He could keep his ministerial credentials if he agreed not to perform any more such weddings in the future but, if he wanted to continue performing gay weddings, he needed to voluntarily surrender his ministerial credentials. The jury gave Rev. Schaefer a month to pray about his decision and come to the Board of Ordained Ministry with his answer.

Rev. Schaefer came back a month later to a gathering at the Conference office and said that he would not promise to refrain from doing gay weddings, nor would he withdraw from ministerial office. The Board of Ordained Ministry, at the direction of the chancellor of the denomination, removed his ministerial credentials upon hearing his decision. Per our rules, I was not to be in that room for that meeting, but I was told that the board members prayed and many openly wept. It was another heart-wrenching moment in this unending saga of pain.

Afterwards, more letters and phone calls of rage poured into my office from the progressive side of the house, not so much communication from the conservative folks. A few supportive calls came from bishop colleagues. My spouse was my greatest help through it all.

But this was a lonely journey, a moral injury. There are times when all we can do is depend on God, who carries all our sorrows and griefs, and this was certainly one of mine.

7

"SMOLDERING ASH"

When I was a child, I walked on a construction site near my home one quiet summer evening. Unbeknownst to me, the white ash pile I climbed on had been a debris fire a few hours before. The fire had stopped burning, but the ashes remained extremely hot. They burned through my sneakers, causing severe burns and blisters on my feet and it took months for me to fully recover.

And that's how it was after the Schaefer Trial. The fire of the trial had ended, but the ashes were still smoldering. Mr. (formerly Rev.) Frank Schaefer became a symbol for the cause of marriage equality in the United Methodist Church. He traveled around the country speaking about the trial. He wrote a book, and there was a stage play written about it that was performed locally. Still later, a documentary movie was produced and shown around the country. His was a compelling story about a pastor's love for his son and a call for the church to rethink its position.

"SMOLDERING ASH"

With each of his appearances, hot coals of criticism continued to come my way, and I found it difficult to fend off the constant calls from the press asking for statements and responses. I remember after one interview the reporter said, "You're not such a terrible person after all, Bishop. I thought you were a monster." I had become the symbol of the system that discriminated against the homosexual community.

I bought a poster of Elsa, the tall blond princess in the blue dress from the Disney movie *Frozen* and hung it up in the office. It proclaimed in bold letters the lyrics of the movie's hit song, *Let it Go!* To "let it go" was an act of focus, patience, and prayer. I was grateful for the faithful support of my spouse, cabinet, clergy friends, and administrative assistant. Also, the Annual Conference director of communications was fair and measured in his responses to the press.

<hr>

Next came the appeal process. Mr. Schaefer's counsel took the penalty stage of the case to the Northeastern Jurisdictional Committee on Appeals for a ruling. Schaefer's legal team argued that a penalty could not be contingent on future behavior. The trial court asked him to promise never again to perform a gay marriage. The appeals committee heard the case in June of 2014 and ruled that Mr. Schaefer had been wrongly defrocked and ordered that we reinstate him immediately and pay back all the salary and benefits he would have earned had he been still serving a church. This also meant this newly reinstated minister had claim on a new pastoral appointment. There were more news reports, press conferences, emails, and phone calls when all of this was announced.

The appointive cabinet and I were willing and ready to offer Rev. Schaefer an appointment to serve a local church in our conference, but at just about the same time I received a call from a United Methodist bishop in California requesting Rev. Schaefer's official transfer to that Conference. This colleague offered Rev. Schaefer a position as a campus chaplain, and he accepted the offer; I agreed, and there was a press conference announcing this new assignment: Rev. Schaefer would continue his ministry as an ordained elder on the west coast.

All the while this trial was happening, both my parents were dying. Mom and Dad had been in skilled nursing care for some time in Baltimore, and they had been slowly declining for a few years. When I wasn't working or fending off reporters, I was driving down to Baltimore to see them, with much grief in my heart. Dad had dementia and died just before the trial began, and Mom passed away a few months afterwards of complications from pneumonia. Losing a parent is heart-wrenching any time, but with the backdrop of the current turmoil it was doubly hard. And losing both parents within months was a triple play.

My parents were people of their generation: hard-working, church-attending, honest, and theologically conservative. They never thought much about sexual orientation as being a part of the spectrum of human diversity. They believed that gay people had made a choice to be so. The church of their day taught that the Bible forbids homosexuality, and Dad's military service during World War II reinforced that in his way of thinking as well.

Many people in the United Methodist Church are like my parents. They are not narrow-minded hate mongers (as some might characterize them). Certainly some extremely conservative people can be mean-spirited and judgmental, but that is true of extremely progressive people as well. Many of the seniors who attended the churches I served were like my parents. They scratched their heads over all of this and simply could not understand why anyone would want to be gay. They hate seeing this firestorm of controversy happening in their peaceful houses of worship.

At the Eastern Pennsylvania Annual Conference gathering in May of 2014, there was left-over unhappiness about the gay wedding that had been performed at the Philadelphia church shortly before the Schaefer trial. Some were demanding that those pastors be formally charged for breaking the covenant of the *Book of Discipline*, and they were furious that I had not done so already. By the end of the Conference, I was presented with a formal complaint signed by sixty pastors charging the banned wedding ceremony participants with chargeable offenses.

Processing that complaint was another unhappy ordeal for me. It was eventually resolved through the help of mediation and conversation. Much against my will, I agreed to take "swift and significant" action if anything like this happened again. This was a moral injury for me, but I felt it was far better than another impasse that would have led to another trial.

Word of my swift-and-significant language got around, and a rash of new unhappy mail began appearing in my mailbox and my email in-box. A group of progressive folks came to my office and there were so many of them that we had to meet in the conference center parking lot for their formal presentation. They brought a large book containing hundreds of signatures imploring me never to allow another trial. I stood there with this contingent and listened to their speeches, received their book, and said thank you.

In the fall of that year, the counsel for the church (the pastor who served as the prosecutor at Rev. Schaefer's trial) took the decision of the Jurisdictional Appeals Committee to the Judicial Council of the United Methodist Church for a ruling. He and his allies were hoping that our highest court would overturn the reversal and once again Rev. Schaefer would be de-frocked.

This did not happen. The Judicial Council upheld the Appeals Committee ruling, the progressive folks claimed another victory, and the conference paid a large sum in legal fees. When it was all said and done, the entire process including the trial, the numerous professional fees, the complaint against the mass-wedding pastors, the judicial counsel process and the pastor's reimbursed compensation cost the conference around $300,000.

The Council of Bishops of the denomination wrote a book that year entitled *Finding Our Way Forward*. It was a collection of articles written by several of our prominent bishops, which offered some solutions to our debate over sexual orientation and same-gender weddings. The book offered diverse perspectives in short, thoughtful chapters. It ended with a call to prayer by the bishop most renowned for his spirituality, Bishop Rubin Job. In this closing chapter he called for the church to put a brake on the fighting and to devote time to prayer and seeking God's will.

I bought 600 copies of the book and gave one to each pastor our Conference. In the fall of that year, I traveled to eighteen different sites to discuss the book with groups of pastors and laity. The pastors shared in small groups. The laity sessions were town-hall meetings with a good bit of grand-standing and Bible quoting. There was little progress in the way of peacemaking at these gatherings.

It was also personally upsetting for me to receive a formal letter from the Camping and Retreats Board of the United Methodist Church expressing their displeasure that the Schaefer trial had been held at a camp. I love our camps! I volunteered at church camp personally throughout my entire ministry, even as a bishop. It was never my intention to show disrespect for camping by holding the trial there. (People were indignant about many things during this battle.)

Many nights at the church camps while serving as a pastor in Baltimore, I sat around campfires with Deaf children and toasted marshmallows. After the fire died to glowing embers and we put the remaining fire out with a bucket of water, I reminded the campers never to step on the ashes. They could get burned.

8

"PRECIOUS SECRET"

The first time I met my future husband was at a backyard picnic for incoming students at Asbury Theological Seminary in Wilmore, Kentucky, on September 4, 1977. I was twenty-three years old, and Michael was twenty-two. My first impression of him was that he was a skinny guy from Texas, and I did not think much more about him than that.

After we had our fill of hot dogs and hamburgers, cooked over the backyard grill at the parsonage of one of the upper classmen, we all sat on the floor in the living room and played an ice-breaker game. This game involved passing around a roll of toilet paper. We were instructed to take "as much as you needed," which got an immediate twitter of nervous laughter. No other explanation was allowed to be given. Some people took one slot of toilet paper, others took several. Since we did not know what was going to happen next, I decided to pull off a very long string of paper, which got some good-natured laughs.

When everyone had taken what "they needed," the leader explained that we were now to tell one thing about ourselves for every slot of toilet paper we had taken. I was sorry I had taken so much, but being the extrovert that I am, it was not hard to give numerous facts about myself. People got to know more about me than those who had only chosen a few slots, but it was all part of the winsomeness of the game. The whole evening was light-hearted and fun for a group of homesick twenty-something young people who were beginning a new life at the seminary.

One of the facts I shared about myself during this toilet paper game was my birthday. "I was born on Beethoven's birthday," I announced, and never gave the actual date. A few weeks later, the skinny guy from Texas, who happened to sit behind me in the Introduction to the Bible 101 class, told me that he also was born on Beethoven's birthday. I gave him such a skeptical look that he produced his driver's license, which indeed revealed a December 16 birthdate.

***

That was the beginning of a conversation that continued into the fall. Our first date was at the Kentucky State Correctional Institution in Lexington for the Friday night Bible study we seminary students taught. Michael and I seemed to have a great deal in common, and it was not

"PRECIOUS SECRET"

long before we were clearly an item on campus, walking arm in arm. Michael would go with me to Lexington every Sunday, where I played the organ at the Tate's Creek Christian Church. They called him the "organist's friend."

By Halloween we were sure that we were meant for each other, and we agreed to get married as we sat under the large yellow gingko tree in front of the seminary administration building. Michael met my parents at Christmas time, we got engaged in March of the following year, I met his parents in May, and we were married on August 19, 1978, not quite a year after we first met. Michael was bright, caring, committed to ministry, and we loved each other very much. There has never been a day in my life that I did not love this "skinny guy from Texas."

Sometimes, however I would have a curious feeling that there was something about him that I did not know. I even said it to him a few times, "There is something inside of you that is a secret." He would just smile and never acknowledge my comment one way or the other. He was a quiet, gentle, and kind person, but occasionally for almost no reason he would have an outburst of anger over some tiny thing. It never seemed that the anxiety-producing incident matched the fury of the rage. It was as if he had an occasional need to let off steam in an uncharacteristic wave of hostility that would go as quickly as it came. There was rarely an apology or an explanation. It was one more thing about Michael I thought was a mystery.

THE EVER-EXPANSIVE SPIRIT OF GOD

We graduated from seminary together on May 30, 1980, and began ministry in two separate rural multiple-point circuits. We were both ordained as Elders in the Baltimore Washington Conference of the United Methodist Church together in 1981, had two lovely sons, and journeyed happily in life, raising a family, serving our churches, paying the bills, visiting the out-of-state families for summer vacations. The years simply flew by. I barely remember a time we had any serious disagreements about anything. Our styles of ministry were different but complimentary, and we had much support and love from family, friends, and church members.

I was the bubbly, outgoing people-person in ministry, and Michael was the studious Bible teacher and youth worker. My sermons were short and full of stories. His were longer and deeply theological, with almost no personal testimonies. For a while we served separate charges, then we served together for eight years while the children were young at my home church, Lansdowne United Methodist Church. A few years later I began serving at the Christ United Methodist Church of the Deaf, and Michael was appointed to Wesley Memorial United Methodist Church for eight years. Then to our great surprise, he was re-appointed to serve my home church, Lansdowne. All the while, I continued serving the Deaf congregation for a total of twenty years.

"PRECIOUS SECRET"

I always thought it was odd that Michael did not relate to people better. We got along fine, and he was close with his family, but he did not have any personal friends. Michael was quiet and friendly, but not relational. I surmised that it was because he was raised in a military family, and they had to move sixteen times while he was in grade school. His immediate family and especially some cousins were his closest friends. On the other hand, I was steeped in rootedness, growing up in a community that went back three generations on both sides of my family. How could Michael ever have learned the people-skills that I acquired from my family of origin and my many long-term school friends?

He commented sometimes that he never liked the boy classmates while he was growing up, as they were too rough for him. He would sometimes be teased and bullied for not being more of a macho guy. Sports, hunting, cars, drinking, and "scoring" with women were not his interests. On several occasions, he would say to me "I hate men," and though he related well-enough to his male church members and male colleagues in ministry, he was never close with any of them.

More than anything else on earth, Michael loved to read. He had all kinds of books and hardly a week would pass without another book arriving in the mail. He was like a walking dictionary if you ever needed to know anything. He was Google before there was Google, with a vast

THE EVER-EXPANSIVE SPIRIT OF GOD

amount of knowledge in his head. A curious thing about his reading material was that he had a huge collection of books about women: women's brains, women's anatomy, women's history, and women's sexuality. I always thought it was a bit strange, but I figured he was just trying to understand *me* better. There was never any pornography or unfaithfulness, just many books about women. *That was nice*, I thought.

One year, at the children's Christmas play at church, they needed a cast member who would play the part of an old woman. When the frazzled Sunday School teacher could not find a woman to volunteer to play the part, she asked Michael to do it. He agreed, and people raved about his performance. Afterwards the Sunday School teacher exclaimed that he was better than Robin Williams in the movie *Mrs. Doubtfire* (a movie about a man who dressed as a woman to be hired as the nanny for his own children after he and his wife had divorced). *That was nice*, I thought.

Then there was a church youth group fund-raiser when Michael promised to dye his hair pink and purple if they raised a certain amount of money for their mission project. The kids promptly raised enough money so they could force their beloved youth-leader pastor to dye his hair. The victorious teenagers marched into our kitchen with bottles of pink and purple hair dye and soon there was a strange glow in Michael's blond locks. In a skit on Rally Sunday, the youth also painted his fingernails. He was such a good sport, always willing to do anything for

"PRECIOUS SECRET"

those kids, and he certainly seemed to enjoy it. *That was nice*, I thought.

When I was elected bishop in 2008, our life changed radically. I was absorbed with my episcopal duties and Michael filled in at a church whose pastor had suddenly taken ill during my first year. He also served quite a few other part-time, short-term pastorates in my Conferences as needed during my tenure. Life was one continuous blur of activities for me, but for Michael it simply meant there was more time for contemplation and reading. We had many opportunities to travel together on various international mission trips and meetings of the Council of Bishops, attending numerous banquets, church dedications, conferences, church anniversary celebrations, and workshops locally and in other states.

One of our out-of-state trips was to a leadership summit in Utah in 2010, held at an exclusive country club resort. To enter this venue, one had to take a tram straight up the side of a steep mountain range. The view was spectacular. Each sleeping room had its own fireplace and a butler who turned the bed down each night and put a foil-covered chocolate on the pillows. The event was for bishops and pastors of the largest 100 churches in the United States. One of the 100 largest churches in the country happened to be in the Eastern Pennsylvania Conference and the pastor of that church, his wife, and Michael and

THE EVER-EXPANSIVE SPIRIT OF GOD

I went together to this exotic locale. It was a rich educational learning experience, and I enjoyed meeting these super-star pastors of the denomination.

One evening after a long day of classes, Michael said he had something to tell me. We sat by the marble fireplace in our luxury hotel room, and he said a most amazing thing: "Peggy, I have come to the realization that I am a woman."

I can't remember much else he said that evening, because at that moment of revelation the shock of his news drowned out most of the conversation. I do remember that he promised he would not dress like a woman in public or come out to the world while I was serving as an active bishop.

I pushed on with my bishop life and refused to deal with it. I was in deep denial at first and hoped the situation would simply go away. What would people say if they found out that the bishop's spouse was a woman? Would that make me a lesbian? Would there be formal charges lodged against me for living in a same-sex marriage? What would our families think?

Several months later, however, I finally decided to talk further with Michael about this transgender reality and this time I listened carefully. It seemed that he had always felt different growing up. His sister got to take ballet lessons and wear frilly clothes, and he wanted to do those

"PRECIOUS SECRET"

kinds of things; but he knew it wasn't gender appropriate. Michael's father sometimes encouraged him to join sports teams, which he did not enjoy. He did not feel comfortable with who he was as a male. He knew his real self was invisible to everyone, including me, and he had nowhere to go with this incongruent gender reality. Michael knew these kinds of conversations were dangerous and there was no safe place to discuss it, so he bottled it all up inside himself for a long, long time.

Michael told me that marrying me felt like the right thing to do because he loved me, and I loved him, and he always wanted to have a family. Clarity about his gender identity was still in an undeveloped state at that time. Michael was always an exceptional husband and father, caring and loving in every way. With years of discernment and introspection, though, he had come to a full understanding of his female gender identity, and he knew it was not going to go away. I needed to accept this and work with him about it. The challenge was living in this high-profile profession and keeping this precious secret.

9

"PINK TIGHTS"

From this point onward, I will refer to my spouse, Michael, as "Mary" and use the pronouns of she/her/hers. She chose the name Mary because of a dream she had in which God invited her to give birth to a daughter. This was a recurring dream for Mary, and when she finally accepted the invitation it was a confirmation that she herself was the daughter she was to give birth to. That is when she moved forward with telling me about her transgender reality. Mary, the mother of Jesus, was likewise invited by God to give birth, and thus the name "Mary" became her choice.

One day I was shopping at an outlet mall and saw a pair of hot-pink tights in the window of clothing store that caters to large-sized women. I decided to buy them for Mary. Up until now, she had not done much about transitioning. Though we had talked about it from time to time, but there had been little progress in Mary's transition, and I suspected that my hesitancy was part of the reason. In my heart, I wanted to support her honest reality, but I was terrified at the same time. I had come to believe that all the mysterious things about Mary that I had experienced in our thirty-two years of marriage began to make sense. When I got the sudden urge to buy a pair of hot pink tights, I knew it could be a tiny sign of affirmation and that it was time for us to take the next steps.

"Here is something for you," I announced and tossed the Lane Bryant store bag into her hands as I came home from shopping. She was quite pleased with the outrageous color and immediately tried them on, but I had bought a size that was far too big. Mary was much smaller than I thought, and we had a good laugh together! That was the beginning of her trying out women's clothes. She went to the local Good Will thrift store and bought lots of used women's attire. Some did not fit so well, but she felt she couldn't use the fitting room in the store. Sometimes her choice of style was contrary to my taste; but it was her decision, not mine. It was all a part of Mary's journey of becoming a woman and the beginning of my role as a fashion consultant.

THE EVER-EXPANSIVE SPIRIT OF GOD

Slowly, Mary and I began to talk more and more about this "transgender thing," as I called it. I read several books about it, including books written by women like me who had transwomen spouses. I discovered how tragic and dangerous the trans world is for many. Transmen and transwomen are twice as likely to be murdered or raped than any other population. Their suicide rate is also double that of the national average according to some studies. It is particularly hard on female trans folk, that is, those who change from female to male, as there is a bias against effeminate men in our society. Tomboy females who transition to male fare somewhat better, but it is difficult for both genders.

I learned many other things from books. When someone comes out as transgender, they must be ready to lose everything: their job, their family, their marriage, their friends, everything precious. Often that is exactly what happens. Many marriages fail and many families refuse to have anything to do with their family member who comes out. Some spouses won't even allow their own children to be around their own mother or father.

Our world is so wired to be binary in its understanding of gender that when people believe their true self is living in the wrong body it is difficult for others to understand or accept. Some people think that transgender people are the same as gay people, cross-dressers, drag queens, or even sexual predators stalking in public bathrooms. There is much ignorance and unfounded fear and sadly, the church can be one of the worst places of all. People often quote the Bible verse, "Man and woman God created them," from Genesis 5:2 and conclude that trans folks are transgressing God's created order and believe this is a sin.

Years ago, people who came out as transgender were put in mental institutions. It is only in the last twenty years that gender diversity is beginning to be understood as part of the spectrum of human experience. In addition, there is a wide variety of people in the transgender community. *Gender non-conforming* people are neither male nor female. Some are *gender fluid,* floating between genders in their self-expression. Others are *a-gender,* which means they express no gender identity at all. There are also physically intersexed people and a host of other categories. Each person is unique. The *cisgender* world (those whose body and sense of gender identity are congruent since birth) sometimes do not easily understand or accept this reality.

In time, Mary sought professional counseling and searched the Internet to find someone who specialized in this field. Going online is a valuable resource for people who live in the transgender closet. It is a place to find out vast amounts of information about that community without self-disclosure. There are numerous private websites and chatrooms dedicated solely to this niche of life. Some of the websites are more political, as this has become truly a human rights concern. Other sites are dedicated solely to information, services, and support. Some explain the fine details of how to tell family and friends and how to navigate difficult issues such as using a public restroom.

Mary engaged in therapy (with a transwoman counselor) for about a year. To transition physically and legally in this country, a person must have a certification from two licensed professionals that they are of a sound mind and have thought through all the aspects of a gender transition.

Mary and I went together for one of her therapy sessions. The counselor presented as female in dress and hairstyle, but her voice was low and something about her appeared masculine. Of course, that is what one would expect. I simply needed to get used to this as I worked through my still uncomfortable feelings. We talked about living in the closet, about our married life, and about the on-going controversy in the United Methodist Church over homosexuality. She questioned why I would even stay in this position as a bishop with a transwoman spouse. I wondered that myself at times. Living in the closet is not easy, but if we were outed there would surely be credibility concerns about my leadership and integrity.

I also sought professional counseling for myself with a woman who specialized in transgender family therapy. She worked with adults but also with children and teens who are questioning their gender identity or helping their

"PINK TIGHTS"

parents navigate the often confusing and sometimes contentious political world of school bathrooms, hormone blockers, and sports team protocols. There are increasing numbers of young people with gender dysphoria, which can lead to a serious form of depression.

I did not have answers for many of the questions my therapist asked. Some days I still wished it would all go away, and some days it was a fascinating adventure into a totally obscure planet of tenacious, freedom-loving people. My background in Deaf and disability ministry taught me well about the giftedness and determination of people on society's margins. This was also an important justice issue that society and the church needed to address so that transgender people could have recognition, respect and equality like everyone else. I had to keep positive and quell the voices of fear inside. My therapist was a great help in that regard.

In time, there was an appointment with an endocrinologist where Mary was prescribed hormone therapy. Mary's counselor recommended a particular doctor and sent the documentation verifying that Mary was psychologically ready to begin using female hormones. In the trans-world there are doctors, hairstylists, electrolysis technicians, and massage therapists who are trans-friendly. It is wise to use professionals who have earned a name for themselves as being open on this issue because they can and will provide the services requested without judgment or rejection.

THE EVER-EXPANSIVE SPIRIT OF GOD

―

Mary absolutely loved the inner feeling she experienced from being on estrogen (the female hormone). Her body and her soul had finally come together from the inside out. I had never seen her so happy and talkative all the years I had known her. I wanted to be happy with her and to some extent I was. But it was like living in a strange dream at times. Things were normal in many day-to-day ways, but at the same time things would never be the same.

I remember one night Mary came to bed wearing a feminine pink nightgown and I suddenly felt a rush of anger inside. *I am the female in this house! I did not sign up for this!* were some of the thoughts I was feeling at that moment, but I never said it aloud. I did not want to hurt Mary. I just laid in bed, silent tears streaming down my face and onto the pillow. *Yet how can I deny this great joy my beloved was experiencing?* I decided that night that I had to live one day at a time, and that is how it went. We kept living together and things slowly got better. Eventually, this began to be our new normal, and sometimes it was even fun!

Mary grew her hair long and painted her fingernails. When her hair got long enough for a ponytail, I was relieved because many middle-aged men have ponytails, and her bushy mass of gray/blond hair was a bit odd-looking without the ponytail. Also, when her long fingernails got brittle and split from the nail polish, she decided not to have long nails anymore and I was relieved about that too. Even though I was now inwardly accepting, I still did not want anyone to suspect anything.

However, we did let a few people know about this secret. We told a trusted retired bishop and our spiritual directors (who were very supportive), as well as our two adult sons. Our sons were not too surprised, as they had noticed the physical changes in their father; another clue was her constant posting of transgender information on Facebook. We spent time talking about it for months afterwards. It was helpful for them to know that their dad's presentation in public would remain male for the time being.

During that same time, Mary went to Moravian Theological Seminary for two years and earned a Certificate in Spiritual Direction. She did some direction work with an inmate at the state prison, wrote wonderful liturgies for Holy Communion services, and taught classes for the United Methodist Women's Mission U summer schools. She stopped serving as an interim pastor in local churches for a while, and this seemed to be a good decision overall. There was less of a chance of people finding out this way. Life went on. God's grace covered us through it all.

Mary attended the annual Keystone Transgender Conference in Harrisburg, Pennsylvania, each year and would present in public as a woman at the event, which was held at a large downtown hotel. She taught courses on spirituality in the transgender context and was asked to present every year. Every time she left the house for these conferences, with her suitcase full of women's clothing, I prayed that no one would figure out that she was the spouse of a bishop. She did meet a lay man from one of my churches who had a son who had transitioned, but nothing bad came of it.

Mary also gave a lecture about ministry with transgender people at a Clinical Pastoral Education class at a local Veteran's Hospital. Blessedly, no one who met the female version of my spouse ever made a public spectacle about it while I was serving as an active bishop. The trans world and their allies are often protective, as they well know the dire cost of being outed. For that we were grateful. But more was still to come.

10

"SURGERY"

Mary prayerfully decided to have surgery at the recommendation of her endocrinologist, who had been prescribing hormone therapy for some time. This would lessen the need for testosterone blockers. Though not what they call a full "bottom surgery," it was the next right step on the journey.

The day for this procedure was January 20, 2016. I drove Mary to an outpatient surgical center in Philadelphia. It was a gray and bitterly cold day, and it felt like we were walking off a cliff. Mary had prepared for this day for many years, but it still was a bit scary for her. The procedure had been approved by two therapists as required by the World Professional Association for Transgender Health (WPATH) standards of care, and the surgeon was a well-known physician in the trans-world.

I sat in the waiting room aimlessly flipping through magazines while the surgeon operated, and then I was called to the recovery room when she woke up from the anesthesia. All the nurses called her "Mary," and this was the first time I heard her new name spoken in public. Thankfully, everything had gone well and we were given detailed instructions about post-operation care and she was released. We drove home with those gray clouds still hanging over us. Mary spent the day in bed.

In the middle of the night, she got up and then fell to the floor because of some sudden sharp pain spasm and laid there for a long time. I tried to get her up, but I was not able to lift her even a little. I thought I would have to call 911, but she finally sat up and slowly crawled back into bed. This was all rather frightening and lonely. Although we had told our children and a few select people about her transitioning, we kept this surgery completely confidential.

Over the weekend there was a twenty-four-inch blizzard. The day that Mary's stitches were scheduled to be removed at the doctor's office, the world was buried in snow. It was so deep that the plows that usually came to our house to dig us out were overwhelmed with other jobs. Our garage was completely snowed in, and I spent hours shoveling a small walking path from the front door to the street, where a township plow had moved enough snow for a single lane of traffic. Miraculously, I found a

"SURGERY"

cab that was willing to drive us to Philadelphia on these treacherous roads.

Ironically, the cab driver, whose name was Jennifer, appeared to me to be a transwoman. I kept thinking I was imagining this, but with all the reading I had been doing I was more aware of the markers. I was also thoroughly convinced she was an angel sent our way on that perilous journey into the city on roads that were barely passable. Jennifer's cab was the tenth taxi company I had called that morning. Jennifer even stayed and waited for us during the appointment so she could drive us back home!

During the days that followed, Mary experienced one round of bladder infections after another. She took several rounds of antibiotics, but it seemed like no medication could combat these tenacious infections. Strangely enough, I had a bladder infection around the same time. Being sick and homebound by piles of snow that wouldn't melt due to unusually frigid temperatures made our lives seem even more difficult. There was no one to talk to about this except God.

Blessedly, within a few weeks Mary had healed, the infections passed, and the sun came out once again.

In the meantime, transgender politics were swirling around the country with landmark discrimination laws passed in North Carolina that denied transgender people equal rights. This cost the state many contracts with sports teams, rock concerts, and conventions, as there was a national backlash against this discrimination. Then President Obama signed an executive order that protected transgender people's rights and allowed them to get health care benefits under the Affordable Care Act. The United States military also began policies that required acceptance for their transgender workforce, including health care benefits. Some public schools began providing gender-neutral bathrooms and other gender-affirming options for transgender students.

The Olympics athlete Bruce Jenner came out as transgender and appeared on the cover of *Vogue* magazine as Caitlyn Jenner, and there was a series of reality-TV episodes about her dramatic transition. Another series, *Transparent* was aired on Amazon Prime television. This was the story of a transwoman who came out to her family of young adult children. The TV series *Orange is the New Black* featured a professional transwoman actress, Laverne Cox.

It seemed like the whole world was focusing on transgender people everywhere I turned. Oddly enough, the issue kept coming up in the life of my churches on a regular basis as well. First, there was a worried grandmother with a trans adult grandson pouring out her heart to me that she wanted him to go back to being a female. Then there was a trans-female seminary student trying to find a denomination that would ordain her. After that, a trans-male graduate student from one of my churches contacted me about our ordination process. That summer at one of

"SURGERY"

my Annual Conferences, a pastor gave a testimony about her brother who had transitioned.

There were issues with children coming up as well. I heard from a family in one of my congregations with a child who kept telling his parents that he was really a girl. One of my pastors had a young adult daughter who was transitioning. In all these cases, I would listen and make no more comment than was necessary. Sometimes I would suggest a book or a DVD to watch. Occasionally I would meet with a person or a family in my office and be a compassionate ear. People were always surprised how knowledgeable I was about the topic.

One of saddest moments for me was in a meeting with pastors and lay people that year who were concerned about the issue of homosexuality in the church. Some of them wanted the church to remain closed to ordination and marriage rights for trans people as well as gay people. I had done many of these meetings before, but at this one a man began talking at great length, ranting that transgender people were frivolously switching genders "each day" and forcing the government to create laws to accommodate the "fifty varieties of genders they claimed to have." This gentleman warned the group with great passion that the church would soon have to close all their bathrooms because of "these people." I just stood there listening, silently screaming inside, *YOU DON'T GET THIS AT ALL!*

It became clear to me that the church was not a safe or accepting place for people who are transgender. Misinformation and ignorance abounded, and within the walls of the churches there was negativity about this increasingly visible phenomenon.

⁓

Spring came early the year of Mary's surgery. On one warm day we bought some new spring clothes for her at a department store (not the Good Will), yet her life for the most part remained in the closet. Often when we would go into stores or to a restaurant together, however, people working in the shops would say, "Can I help you ladies?" Mary was always pleased to hear these gender-affirming greetings, and it was clear to me she had made a good and healthy decision for her life.

11

"GENERAL CONFERENCE 2016"

The quadrennial legislative gathering of the United Methodist Church, known as the "General Conference" was held in Portland, Oregon, in May of 2016. Portland is known as "The City of Roses," but the meeting was not altogether rosy. At this ten-day gathering, the laws of the *Book of Discipline* were once again reviewed, revised, and amended. We also perfected our *Book of Resolutions*, which is an ever-changing tome of all things that United Methodists believe about a plethora of social issues.

Bishops sit in the front on the stage at the conference but do not vote or have any influence over the legislative process. Bishops also preside over this business meeting and have to handle the nuances of Parliamentary procedure with its numerous amendments, questions, and "points of order."

THE EVER-EXPANSIVE SPIRIT OF GOD

I volunteered to offer sign language interpreting for the "Episcopal Address," which was given by Bishop Gregory Palmer of the West Ohio Conference. It was fun to be in that limelight offering my hands of a bishop to tell the Deaf people there what another bishop was saying. I also was invited to lead one of the noon-day Communion Services and the theme was "disabilities." There was an overflow crowd, including people from the disability community in attendance as well as those who were providing service to the delegates with disabilities at the gathering.

Throughout the conference, I had time to chat with the disability leadership. They were one of the most "voiceless" justice committees in the denomination. Years earlier, things had been so much better for the disability committee. With shrinking dollars and shrinking interest from the major programmatic agencies of the denomination, their voice and their program budgets had dwindled. (Two years after this conference, the Disability Committee would be eliminated altogether from the mission board's budget and was left to raise their own funds.)

The choir from the Christ UMC of the Deaf, my former parish in Baltimore, came to bring a few songs in sign language at this event. It was so good to see them all, and I shed some tears as I greeted them at the conference. I had brought this same choir to General Conference three

"GENERAL CONFERENCE 2016"

other times in the past. Even after eight years, it was still amazing to me that I was no longer directly serving this congregation.

General Conference is historically a place where strong and painful demonstrations about the acceptance of homosexuality and gay marriage takes place every four years, and in preparing for this event there was every expectation that this would be the biggest show-down of all. Since 1972, the *Book of Discipline* continued to contain prohibitions about homosexual people in ordained ministry and banning same gender marriage ceremonies. Every General Conference I attended (since 1996) included large demonstrations and sometimes acts of civil disobedience, loud protests, and even physical altercations with law enforcement and arrests.

At the 2000 General Conference in Cleveland, Ohio, a group of progressive folks had taken the stage during a plenary session and were arrested by the police and led away in handcuffs. Among the arrested were two United Methodist bishops. At that same event, an emotionally distraught woman threatened to jump off the balcony in an attempted suicide. People physically restrained her, but the anxiety of that moment haunted the rest of the conference.

In recent years the acceptance of homosexuality had become more of a social justice issue in the United States and the pressure was building for this denomination to take a new look at their 40-year-old restrictive policies. The Supreme Court had legalized same-gender marriages since we had last met in 2012. Several other mainline denominations in the United States had changed their long-standing conservative policies in favor of more liberal leanings that permitted ordination and church marriages of gay and lesbian people.

Numerous complaints in our United Methodist churches were filed against pastors who had performed same-gender marriages or had themselves came out as gay or lesbian. It was becoming untenable for bishops to handle all of these complaints with the current official policies. No one knew that better than me.

This was the first General Conference since the well-publicized "Schaefer trial" I had initiated in Eastern Pennsylvania, and around the country other cases had gotten much publicity: but none had gone to a full trial except the one in my conference. Each subsequent case was dismissed or resolved in favor of the liberal side of the house. There was therefore grief and disappointment in the hearts of conservative congregants and pastors, and they brought this pain with them to the conference as well.

Rev. Frank Schaefer's movie about his trial had made the rounds in various places across the country in preparation for General Conference. It was hoped that this compelling story of the love of a father for his son could turn the tide of sympathy toward more progressive legislation from the delegates. As expected, large groups of progressive people came to the conference to stage demonstrations. They were clad in colorful rainbow shirts, vests, and stoles, and they carried banners and signs that called for equality and acceptance.

I walked by one group of demonstrators who were marching with banners made of the clergy stoles of United Methodist pastors who had formerly been ordained in the church and had either quit or been defrocked because of their orientation or participation in a gay wedding. Someone held out Rev. Schaefer's stole and shook it in my face. I said, "I recall that he is still an ordained pastor," to which the marcher shouted, "But YOU defrocked him!" On another occasion a woman rushed up to me and said with rage, "So YOU are Peggy Johnson!" It was hard for me to support a cause that was so filled with judgmental rage against me personally. I knew it was a product of years of their suffering and rejection and I could understand it, but it still was hurtful.

Several times protests from this group broke out on the floor of the General Conference, and business had to be halted or the starting time delayed. Loud speeches with bullhorns blasting demands for justice rang through the vast convention hall. Sometimes the protestors would line the hallways with signs or stand in rows with duct tape over their mouths symbolizing the way the church had silenced their voices. Conservative people had their meetings too, but quietly at large hotels or churches nearby. Tension between the two groups was high.

THE EVER-EXPANSIVE SPIRIT OF GOD

All the paragraphs from the *Book of Discipline* that concerned homosexuality and same-gender weddings were up for revision at this conference, and there did not seem to be any way that this was going to go well. Some leaders were contemplating the real possibility of a schism at this very conference. The Council of Bishops wanted unity for our beloved church, but we bishops were also divided on this issue, like the rest of those in the denomination.

In what I consider nothing less than a miraculous movement of the Holy Spirit, there came a proposal to the floor of the General Conference that called for the suspension of all debate and voting on the homosexual paragraphs in the *Book of Discipline* and to refer the entire matter for further study. The study would be conducted by a hand-picked commission that would include people from all sides of the theological spectrum, and this conversation would be executed by the Council of Bishops. This small group, to be known as "The Commission for the Way Forward," would perfect the paragraphs in question in the *Book of Discipline* and bring it all back to a specially called session of General Conference before our next regularly scheduled General Conference in 2020.

This proposal was debated long and hard and was defeated. Then this same proposal was brought back again to the floor with a few key revisions, and this time it passed by 23 votes. As the 2016 General Conference ended, we prayed with all our hearts that we could remain a united denomination at the end of this process.

The day after General Conference ended, the bishops met for a full day to discuss what this commission would look like. I never say much at these meetings, but I did go to the microphone and say that we needed to include someone who was transgender on the "Commission for the Way Forward," but this never happened. The executive committee and several other carefully chosen members of the Council were designated to begin to assemble the commission and commence with the work. I volunteered to be a part of the prayer committee that organized prayer events during this season. If we were to stay united as a denomination, it would only be by the supernatural power of God.

12
"ANNUAL CONFERENCES 2016"

The Eastern Pennsylvania Annual Conference held its annual meeting in Lancaster, Pennsylvania, in June of 2016, just a month after the contentious and inconclusive General Conference in Portland. We met at the downtown Marriott Hotel for our venue because we would be using that same hotel to host the Northeastern Jurisdictional Conference the following month. The accommodations provided more comfort and sophistication than the cinderblock warehouse where we usually met. The padded seats and chandelier lighting, however, did not take away the pain of the aftermath of the General Conference and the smoldering division over homosexuality that was still in the air.

"ANNUAL CONFERENCES 2016"

Our conference theme was "racial justice," and we particularly highlighted Native American ministries and held a formal service of repentance at the opening worship service for all the acts of injustice against indigenous people that have occurred in our country. It just happened that the city of Lancaster was the site of a horrific massacre of innocent Native American families in 1763. That summer, Native Americans were in North Dakota protesting the Dakota Access Pipeline, an oil company project that would imperil the water systems and desecrate the native burial grounds in that area. There was pain and grief coming from that ordeal as well during our conference in Lancaster.

The city of Lancaster had a huge population of Latino and Hispanic people at the time (as it does now), and it was known as one of the largest centers for immigrant resettlements in the state and in the nation. Many people lived there in fear for their documentation status as immigrants. The upcoming presidential election in November of 2016 could possibly make things worse. The pain and poverty in the immigration community was also an undertone at the conference.

For the African American community there was the pall of grief and rage over the increasing number of police shootings around the country involving innocent victims who were people of color. In addition, there was a fresh memory of the horrific mass killing a year before

THE EVER-EXPANSIVE SPIRIT OF GOD

of nine African Americans in South Carolina at a Bible study at the Mother Emmanuel African Methodist Episcopal Church. The perpetrator was an angry young white supremist hoping to start a race war. In the basement of the very hotel where we held the conference, there was a museum that included the remains of an Underground Railroad passageway, a reminder of the scourge of slavery in this country.

The LBGTQIA community had just suffered a deadly assault at a gay night club known as "The Pulse" in Orlando, Florida. Fifty people were gunned down in that violent hate crime. We read the names of all the victims at the first session of the conference and the room crackled with silence.

Globally there had been a massacre in the Democratic Republic of Congo, where terrorists came into villages and raped, pillaged and burned the properties of innocent people. In the Philippines, the government was taking over the land of poor farmers because of some dispute over gold. In Europe, thousands of Middle Eastern and African refugees were seeking asylum there because of wars and genocide in their home countries.

It seemed as if the whole world was reeling with injustice, oppression, and violence. Human history has been one long saga of people hating one another because of who they are, what they have, or what they believe. Power and gold seem to be the gods of this planet. The overt oppression of homosexual and transgender people in the church was a part of it all. Could not the church be better than the world and offer hope and acceptance to all oppressed people? But that is difficult to accomplish when people use the Bible to justify oppression and rules in the denominational law book that institutionalize the exclusion.

The ordination service at the conference session that week was held at the nearby First United Methodist Church. It is a cathedral-like edifice with much stained glass, a high vaulted ceiling, and a magnificent pipe organ. All the participants in the conference walked to the church from the hotel in a grand procession. The clergy contingent, vested in white robes with red stoles, were quite an impressive sight walking two by two down the narrow streets.

On either side of the street were people holding signs protesting our denomination's refusal to ordain homosexual people. The signs were calling for justice and inclusion, and many from our churches wearing rainbow stoles were part of the demonstration.

A stranger who was dangerously homophobic joined the crowd on the street. He had a bullhorn and barked loud insults at the protestors saying they were going to hell and that homosexuality was an abomination in the eyes of God. This stranger was also riding an imposing white horse, making the whole scene even more menacing. I felt that at any moment violence could erupt, but blessedly, after the procession ended so did the protest, and the ordination service proceeded, without any further incidence.

I pondered the affect all of this had on those who were presenting themselves for ordination that night. As they knelt before me and I laid my hands on their heads and said the sacred words, "Take authority to preach the Word, administer the Sacraments, and order the life of the church," I wondered what sort of church they would be leading into the future.

⁓

The Peninsula-Delaware Conference, the more conservative of my two conferences, held their Annual Conference a few weeks later. They had one homosexuality-related resolution to debate and vote upon. There were only a few progressive churches in this conference and, though the makers of the resolution did an excellent job presenting their case, the resolution failed by a large majority. It was almost as if this issue did not exist in that part of the world. I experienced the disappointment and hurt that the makers of the motion experienced. I went over to talk to them afterwards but there were no words that I could offer except to "pray for a better day to come."

13

"JURISDICTIONAL CONFERENCE 2016"

Every four years in the summer after the General Conference, each of the five jurisdictions of the United Methodist Church in the United States holds a local conference at the same time across the country. The most important work at this conference has to do with bishops: electing new bishops, assigning bishops to their areas for the next four years, and celebrating the retirement of the bishops who had come to the end of their tenure. Our international Annual Conferences, known as "Central Conferences," have quadrennial local conferences as well, but they are not scheduled for the same week.

Jurisdictional and Central Conferences also include the presentation of various reports, the election of officers and committee members, the setting of the quadrennial budget, and the discussion and debate over social justice resolutions. The 2016 Northeastern Jurisdictional Conference was held in Lancaster, Pennsylvania, and the Eastern Pennsylvania Annual Conference was the gracious host. Lay and clergy delegates from the ten Annual Conferences from the Northeastern part of the United States were in attendance, as well as nine active bishops and fifteen retired bishops and their spouses. Much preparation went into the execution of this conference, and our team worked together well. The worship services were beautiful. Our volunteers in red vests served tirelessly, giving directions, carrying suitcases, and handling all the other "behind the scenes" work that goes into every church conference.

Resolutions about homosexuality were presented at this conference as expected. Each of the resolutions was ruled "out-of-order" by the presiding bishops because they were calling for changes in the *Book of Discipline*, which a local jurisdiction does not have the power to legislate in the United Methodist Church. There was much debate and lively conversation, nonetheless. That was the intent of putting these resolutions forward—to test the waters. It appeared from the "straw votes" that most of the delegates were supporting a more open and inclusive church.

This was a disappointment to the conservative delegates. Some candidly shared with me that they were beginning to feel alienated from their own denomination.

"JURISDICTIONAL CONFERENCE 2016"

In the past the votes had always swung in the conservative direction, but now things were shifting the opposite way. A new day was coming.

Present at the conference were some representatives from a progressive LGBTQIA caucus group. Visitors are allowed at this conference, and folks from this caucus held signs and sang outside of the plenary hall. I engaged them in conversation and promised I would intervene if there was ever a moment of concern with our accommodations. I was afraid of the potential for loud demonstrations and meeting disruptions, but thankfully none occurred.

One of the main resolutions at the conference was a "Call to Action." This would require our jurisdiction to engage on intentional work around eradicating institutional racism against African American people specifically in our conferences and churches. It demanded that white people be held accountable for their use of privilege to maintain institutional power and financial control. A lengthy document was put in place that required all bishops to initiate anti-racism training events, establish new African American churches, recruit and support more African American candidates for ministry, and engage in a host of other practical action steps.

At this conference we elected two new bishops: Bishop Cynthia Moore-Koikoi and Bishop LaTrelle Easterling. Both women were African American and theologically progressive. There had been some late-night secret meetings among some of the Peninsula-Delaware delegates about their moving to the Baltimore-Washington Conference as a two-point charge, but none of this materialized.

I did not feel much enthusiasm from my conference delegates about my being reassigned as bishop for another term when they announced the placements of bishops on the last day. I understood the tepid response, as the normal process is that bishops stay for only two quadrennium (a total of eight years) and I had completed my eight years. Most were expecting that I would be moving to a different area and the Philadelphia Area would be getting a new bishop. I thought that would happen as well. A third four-year term is allowable, but it is not the normal practice.

I was given another term, but I received a directive from the Episcopacy Committee that in the next four years I needed to be "stronger, have more goals, and seek the wisdom of the large membership church pastors to improve my leadership skills." I knew that the continual decline of the churches in the area did not reflect well on my performance, but I was not sure my style of leadership was totally to blame.

I tried very hard to be positive, brave, and happy at the close of this Jurisdictional Conference, but it was purely acting. The convention hall was extremely cold with air conditioning that could never seem to be controlled, the seating of the bishops was such that my chair was in the back by myself, and I was developing an abscessed tooth (one that required surgery the following week). I was so exhausted by the end of it all that I went home and cried for two hours.

～

Other jurisdictions in the United States elected bishops at the same time as the Northeastern Jurisdiction was meeting. Fifteen new United Methodist bishops in the United States were elected by the end of that week. Those elected were more diverse, younger, and mostly theologically progressive. No election got more attention than the elevation of Bishop Karen Oliveto to the episcopacy in the Western Jurisdiction. She was openly gay and legally married. Immediately there were calls from conservative voices for the Judicial Council to weigh in on the legality of this election. That kind of thing takes months and, in the end, Bishop Oliveto was never disqualified when the Judicial Council finally ruled on her electability. (The complainants were from another jurisdiction and had no standing in matters that related to a different jurisdiction.)

Bishop Oliveto was appointed to serve the Mountain Sky Area, which includes Colorado, Montana, Utah, and Wyoming. The Western Jurisdiction tended to be more progressive, and most were quite pleased to have the first openly gay bishop in the United Methodist denomination. Even so, this new leader among us received much hate mail, death threats, and persecution.

Bishop Oliveto was an accomplished theologian, teacher, church pastor and visionary leader. I heard her speak at a Council of Bishops meeting later in the fall of that year. When she spoke, one could sense the presence of Christ in her. She was down-to-earth, personable, and theologically insightful. Her call to ministry story was as genuine and Spirit-filled as any I have heard.

I prayed that the United Methodist Church would put down their swords and shields. The world needs the unified spirit in the church during these times of social upheaval. Trying to stop a justice movement is like trying to stop the wind, and I believed we would be opposing the will of God in doing so. The cause of equal rights for all people ultimately succeeds.

14

"GAY PRIDE PARADE 2017"

I was not intending to go to the Philadelphia Gay Pride Parade on that sunny day in June of 2017. I was not against Gay Pride Parades or the people in my conferences that participated with floats and banners. I just never liked crowds, traffic, or parking hassles in Center City.

I ended up going to the parade quite by happenstance. My spouse, Mary, (still known and presenting as Michael) had been invited to preach at the Old St. George's United Methodist Church in Philadelphia on that day. We arrived early in the morning for the service to find one of the few parking places available on that block of the city! We enjoyed worshiping with this small but vibrant group of people at one of the oldest founding churches of the denomination.

THE EVER-EXPANSIVE SPIRIT OF GOD

Following the service, a member of the church told us that the Gay Pride Parade was within walking distance of the church. He asked if we wanted to go with him. "Sure," I said to the young man, who was an openly gay member of the church, "as long as you lead the way." He was delighted and we hurried down 4th Street and onto Market Street, just as the parade was beginning. My guide explained about the "Gayborhood" (a version of the word *neighborhood*, which was in that part of Philadelphia). Many gay and lesbian people lived on these streets, and they assisted in the planning of this huge annual event that drew people from all over the world.

What we saw was much of what one would expect: a colorful, Mardi-Gras-like celebration with bawdy dancing, loud music, and rainbow colors galore! Marchers in the parade tossed beads and hard candy to onlookers and vendors were selling food (especially Philadelphia cheese steak sandwiches) and souvenirs. What I did not expect were the many floats and marchers who were there as support organizations offering health care, education, family resources, counseling and, yes, spiritual care. There were military folks, doctors, grandmothers, and local politicians.

I saw transgender people marching with pink and blue flags as well. There were some parents walking side by side with their transitioning children. I could only imagine their personal journeys, and what this experience of outward pride and acceptance must have meant to the young lives of these youth.

~

The parade marchers and onlookers were people of all ethnicities, ages, and abilities. Churches and interfaith groups marched by, carrying crosses and symbol of their faith traditions. Their message was simple: "Sharing the love of God with and for all people." I asked my guide to help me find the Eastern Pennsylvania United Methodist churches in the line-up. Mary and I had been standing there for well over an hour and had not seen any of our church people in the parade. Off we went, pushing our way through the crowds to the line-up position, where the groups participating were waiting their turn to march.

We finally located our Eastern Pennsylvania church people, clad in their rainbow-colored shirts with flags and banners, and they were surprised to see us. I was glad that I had come as these were my people doing important justice advocacy. I had always been on their side, despite the church trial, despite the inward turmoil I always experienced about trying to be a bishop to all, despite living in a transgender closet, and despite trying to keep out of the limelight. This was God's work they were doing, and I wanted to be with them.

I posed for a picture with one of my pastors holding a sign that said, "God is Gender Queer—Genesis 1:27." (That is actually a true statement. Genesis 1:27 says, "God created humankind in his image, in the image of God he created them; male and female God created them." So if God's image is male and female then it could be interpreted that God is "gender queer," meaning not man *or* woman but man *and* woman.)

But putting the words *God* and *queer* together will always be scandalous to some, although in fact gender has nothing to do with homosexuality; but in the minds of many theologically traditional people it is one and the same thing. Most of them believed that both are sinful choices and they imagine that God's gender is male and certainly not queer.

⁓

After the parade, I wrote a blog for the Eastern Pennsylvania newsletter about the event, explained what I learned, and posted that picture of me with the Gender Queer sign. It was at that moment that I decided that I simply had to say what I had to say and not be afraid of the push-back anymore.

On June 20, 2017, I posted the following words, "God makes the judgment call at the end of the day. It is not our job. For far too long we have been arguing over particulars, writing resolutions, and speculating about a church schism. All we are being asked to do is simply to love and welcome all people. I encourage all churches to exercise our denominational mandate to be inclusive. There is grace to be found when you meet and listen to the stories

"GAY PRIDE PARADE 2017"

of people where they are—where they live, celebrate, suffer, and struggle daily to gain dignity, human rights, and loving acceptance."

The response from the conservative side of the church was swift and negative. Several pastors and lay people emailed me their disappointment that I even attended this event, much less celebrated it. They also took issue with accepting all people and leaving it to God to do the judging. Their belief that homosexuality was a sin made it difficult for them to be affirming and fully welcoming.

I did get a single, hand-written note from one of the pastors who marched in the parade, thanking me for coming. He will never know how much that meant to me. There was no turning back for me after that day at the Gay Pride Parade.

15

"COMMISSION FOR THE WAY FORWARD"

The 2016 General Conference voted to establish "The Commission for the Way Forward." It was set in motion a few months after the Portland gathering that suspended all decisions concerning homosexuality in favor of this study committee. There were thirty-two people chosen from all over the globe. They included a rich diversity of ethnicities, orientations, ages, and theological perspective. People around this table were clearly not of the same heart, but they persevered in the spirit of unity. In the end they produced three potential options or sketches for solving our impasse over the ordination of gay people and the performance of gay marriages.

"COMMISSION FOR THE WAY FORWARD"

The bishops discussed the Commission's sketches at three Council meetings: November 2017, February 2018, and May 2018. The first was the Traditional Model (in which the *Book of Discipline* was kept the same but enhanced accountabilities would be put in place for people who did not keep the covenant). The second was the Centrist Model (in which all the discriminatory paragraphs in the *Book of Discipline* about homosexuality and the prohibitions against the ordination of gay people and gay weddings would be removed and churches, pastors and annual conferences could choose whatever they wanted to do about it in their context). The third was the Multi-Branch Model (in which there would be essential services of an umbrella denomination but under it would be distinctive branches: traditional, progressive, centrist, and possibly an international branch).

Early on the Traditional Model was eliminated by the bishops because there was a sense that it was essentially what we had currently in the *Book of Discipline* and that was not working for us. Later it was brought back to be included as an option and more work was done to flesh out the meaning of "enhanced accountabilities." It became known as the Traditional Plan. The Centrist Model became known as the One Church Plan and the Multi-Branch Model became known as the Connectional Church Plan.

THE EVER-EXPANSIVE SPIRIT OF GOD

At the Chicago meeting of the Council of Bishops in May of 2018, most of the bishops, including myself, expressed support for the One Church plan. It allowed people in various contexts to minister in a way that was most appropriate for them. It did not change the Constitution of the denomination, and it would keep our current structure with our boards and agencies intact. Many hoped that the One Church plan would be the one and only model brought to the special called session of General Conference in 2019. Some bishops supported one of the other two plans.

The response to the One Church Plan preference of most of the bishops came quickly from the conservative voices in the denomination. The Wesleyan Covenant Association, *Good News* magazine, and other conservative-leaning groups, denounced it, saying plans like this had been proposed by General Conference in the past and had been rejected by the voting delegates. (Which was true, in my opinion.) Not a few unkind things were said about the bishops in some of the articles. At the same time, progressives were also engaging in mean-spirited rhetoric, so clearly civility was long gone.

After the Chicago meeting, I met with the General Conference delegations from both of my Annual Conferences. These were the people who would actually cast a vote at the special called session of General Conference in February of 2019. The One Church Plan seemed to be supported by some, but certainly not by all. The issue of biblical interpretation and covenant-keeping continued to be a concern for the traditional-leaning delegates.

In May of 2018, there was also a Judicial Council meeting to decide if the bishops' preference of the One Church Plan could be the one and only proposal brought to the 2019 special session of General Conference. The Judicial Council ruled that anyone who wanted to bring a plan to General Conference could do so if it was in keeping with the Way Forward initiative.

At the 2018 sessions of my two Annual Conferences that June, we discussed the One Church Plan anyway and I had two speakers at each conference giving the pros and cons and then the conference broke into small groups for table talk. These conversations went surprisingly well with our presenters doing a fine job at making a case for their opinion about the One Church Plan.

There was a resolution at the Eastern Pennsylvania Annual Conference session that proposed as "aspirational" that, if the One Church Plan passed, people who disagreed could leave the denomination and not have to follow what is called the "trust clause" that is part of our United Methodist Church Constitution and leaves all property and assets in the hands of the denomination. Departing local churches must forfeit their buildings and bank accounts if they leave the United Methodist

Church. This exception to the trust clause in effect was proposing that churches could leave the denomination over this issue and *not* have to forfeit their assets if they disagreed with the outcome of General Conference. This resolution was put before the body to test the waters of dissent. It had no real affect; it was just an "aspiration." This resolution failed, but only by a narrow margin.

~

Later at the Peninsula-Delaware session of Annual Conference, a resolution to maintain unity "no matter what happens in 2019 at the special session of General Conference" was placed on the floor for debate and a vote. It was amended to read, "We will maintain unity *if* the *Book of Discipline* stays exactly the same as it is written now." This clearly took a good-spirited call for unity and turned it upside down. Someone called for a secret ballot vote on this amended resolution so that people could vote their true hearts without anyone seeing them raise their hand. When the paper ballots were counted, the amended resolution passed by about twenty votes. Clearly this was a very divided body as well, but it was clearly more evenly divided than in the past. Something was shifting even in the Peninsula-Delaware Conference, which had always been among the most conservative in the UMC.

After that emotional discussion and vote, a young adult lay delegate came to the microphone to announce that she was considering ordained ministry but could not

"COMMISSION FOR THE WAY FORWARD"

be a part of a denomination that excluded the LGBTQIA community. She was one of our brightest and best young people, and I felt the weight of her painful statement as if it was a doomsday prophecy for any denomination that would deny a future to those who are straining for a new day. The young woman continued to speak beyond her three-minute time limit, so the person controlling the microphone cut her off in mid-sentence. It was a chilling moment, but to her credit the young woman kept talking and finished what she had to say without the benefit of amplification. Oddly enough, there was a thunderstorm outside as she spoke, and all we heard was this eerie rumble of thunder.

In November of 2018, the Council of Bishops met at St. Simon's Island, Georgia. A few days before that meeting there was a gathering of the Wesleyan Covenant Association (WCA), a group that supported the Traditional Plan. Three of our residential bishops spoke at this event. The WCA had set up a play book of what they would do if the One Church Plan passed, and it appeared to be schismatic in nature. When the Council of Bishops met at St. Simon's Island later that week, not a word was said about this gathering. Instead, the meeting focused on a review of the various plans and a more in-depth explanation about the Judicial Council rulings in October.

During this gathering we had a time of prayer, and people were asked to go up to those we may have offended and apologize. Most bishops turned to one another and politely passed the peace. Two members of a progressive caucus were sitting in the visitor's section during that service, and I knew I had to be the one to go to them; but I was afraid it would turn out badly. I knelt before these two people and quietly apologized for the pain that our church and I as a bishop had caused them through the years. I was totally ignored; they did not even look at me.

That year there was much flooding in the northeastern part of the country. There were catastrophic fires in California, and devastating hurricanes in the South. It seemed like all of creation was out-of-whack. Nature itself was reeling and crying along with this divided denomination. The church was supposed to be model for grace and unity in this world but it seemed that we were as contentious as secular society. Each side was determined to win no matter the cost at the Special General Conference in 2019.

16

"TOWN HALL MEETINGS 2019"

In the fall of 2018, amid many nights of pouring rain, I drove to fifteen different churches in both of my Annual Conferences for town hall meetings to discuss The Way Forward plans and the upcoming 2019 Special Session of General Conference in February of 2019. Some gatherings were of lay and clergy from a particular district, and some were at local churches that had specific concerns. I accepted every invitation that came my way. Members of the General Conference delegations also spoke at various gatherings, including the ones I was leading.

The crowds were always large and sometimes we even had to set up extra chairs to accommodate the crowd. This had never happened whenever I had come to visit these districts and talk about evangelism or missions. The homosexuality debate had captured the attention of these faithful United Methodists, and at times it seemed to be more important than the overall mission of the church.

~

I showed a PowerPoint presentation about the three plans that were proposed by the Commission for the Way Forward (Traditional, One Church, and Connectional) and explained the timeline for the decision-making process and who would be voting. I never criticized any of the plans, but I also did not deny that I personally supported the One Church Plan. I explained some of the pros and cons of each choice, and the questions and speeches that followed my presentation usually illustrated this clearly. My main goal was to emphasize the vast number of things that we all agreed upon and the importance of unity for the sake of the important mission of the church. In general, these gatherings were civil. Though some of the comments doubtless wounded hearts of people on both sides of the aisle, blessedly there were no protests or outbursts at these events.

From the traditional folks the same questions came up:

- "Suppose the pastor wants to do a same-gender marriage and the church members don't want it to happen in their building, what happens?"
- "Why can't gay people change and become straight?"

- "How can a person call themselves a Christian and be gay?"
- "Why haven't we heard about this until now?" (Many of my pastors did not want to bring this entire matter up because it was divisive. Some pastors never told their members that there was even going to be a Special General Conference in 2019. And some lay people clearly hadn't read any of the materials we had been sending).
- "Can the bishop force us to take a gay pastor in the future?
- "Who elected these people who are going to vote at General Conference?"
- "Can we force the delegates to vote the way we tell them to vote?"
- "The Bible teaches that marriage is only between a man and a woman."
- "The Book of Leviticus says that homosexuality is an abomination, and we must reject people who engage in this lifestyle. We love the sinner and hate the sin."
- "You are going to lose members if we ordained gay people. Our churches are already getting smaller and smaller, and this will finish us off."
- "We are becoming like the world when we accept gay people, and the church is not supposed to compromise on the Word of God."

THE EVER-EXPANSIVE SPIRIT OF GOD

One woman shared with great passion that she had a gay son and, in her mind, he was "spiritually dying every day." She let everyone know that she had totally disowned him because of his sinful choices in life.

The progressive folks brought less questions to these events, and when they stood to speak it was mostly personal or experiential in nature:

- One woman explained that she had visited an Episcopal Church (that had a gay pastor), and the church was alive and vibrant with gay and straight people in attendance. She said it did not stop the church from thriving.
- During several of the gatherings, gay persons would openly share that they were homosexual and that it was not an evil choice on their part, just who they always knew themselves to be all their life.
- Some went on further to explain how they had faithfully served as a layperson in their congregation with excellence and grace. Some felt they were called to be pastors, but the church stood in their way. They loved the church and could not understand why it was rejecting them.
- Some people had gay family members and testified to the goodness of these people and how much the church had hurt them.

"TOWN HALL MEETINGS 2019"

With as much grace as I could muster, I answered the many questions from both sides. I explained the voting process and how delegates were elected at Annual Conference and were supposed to vote their heart and are not bound to vote in a particular way. However, I said, the elected delegates were happy to hear from them and would consider their opinions when making voting decisions. Many followed up and wrote passionate letters to various delegates on both sides of the dispute in the months that followed.

I also stressed that at this special session of General Conference there is the potential for any number of amendments, so at the time of voting there could be a totally new thing presented. This entire debate would all be live streamed through the Internet, so people could watch what was happening in real time. I promised to do more town hall meetings after the General Conference to explain the results of this landmark denominational event.

I explained that churches always set their own wedding policies and that pastors had to respect it. Bishops appoint pastors to congregations that are the best fit possible, and that included theological diversity. I compared it to the many other diversities that the appointive cabinet and I take into consideration when making appointments of clergy to their congregations.

THE EVER-EXPANSIVE SPIRIT OF GOD

I also shared that the One Church Plan would allow every church, pastor, and Board of Ordained Ministry to decide the issues of inclusion locally so that no one would be forced to act against their conscience. For some, the promise of "no pressure to conform" from the One Church Plan was not enough assurance. The possibility that anyone anywhere in our denomination would be allowed to perform a gay person's wedding or ordain a gay person would be grounds for them to leave the church. It had to be all or nothing for many on both sides of the issue.

I learned at these meetings that no amount of biblical interpretation was worth discussing with people of more traditional points of view. The fact that eating shellfish (like shrimp) is considered an "abomination" in Leviticus 11:10 in the Old Testament did not seem to matter to them. They determined that some things still remained an abomination (like homosexuality) and other things (like wearing head coverings in church) were simply now permissible.

The facts that divorce was strongly rejected by Jesus in the Gospel of Matthew (19:3-9) and that he had said not one word about homosexuality did not seem to be a concern to conservatives. In the past, pastors who were divorced (for any reason) had been dismissed in our denomination, but in modern times the church has become more tolerant on that issue. My suggestion that

"TOWN HALL MEETINGS 2019"

"times change, peoples' perspectives change" was totally rejected by them.

I also shared various biblical interpretations over slavery. That did not make a dent either. It seemed that homosexuality was like a big red letter that could never be removed from a person's way of thinking, and that was that. I stopped trying to talk about biblical and historical interpretation after a while.

⁂

It continually rained during that fall. The dismal weather mirrored for me many of these painful town hall meetings. The fear, anxiety, and misinformation that people were expressing was discouraging. It appeared that most of the people in my conferences wanted the *Book of Discipline* to stay the same forever. Across the entire denomination, it appeared that the voting delegates were pretty evenly divided, and it was anyone's guess what people would do when they had the electronic voting pad in their hand at General Conference 2019.

It did surprise me, however, that there were a few tiny glimmers of humor at these meetings. One happened at a town hall event in a rural church. An elderly woman slowly made her way to the microphone and asked, "So if the gays take over, can we still have a rummage sale at the church?" I told her that the church could still have the sale, and she sat down with a pleased look on her face.

Another moment happened at a theologically conservative church where a man stood to give an impassioned speech. "No gay couple will ever, ever, be allowed to be married in front of this altar!" and he pointed to the altar with fire in his eyes. Then he lowered his hand and said, "Well, maybe they can do the wedding in the Sunday School room." I kept a straight face.

17

"IN A RELATIONSHIP"

"Mom, I am calling to let you know that I am in a relationship," said our youngest son, Gabe, who is now age thirty-five.

"It's about time! Tell me all about him," I said.

Gabe and his partner have given permission for their sexual orientation to be shared in this book and since this new relationship started, Gabe is more out than he has ever been. Gabe never denied that he was gay, but he never volunteered the information to people openly or joined any Gay Pride Parades or organizations.

Mary and I always have been fully supportive of him as a gay person. It is who he is! However, we are constantly concerned for him at the same time. Gay people are the target of hate crimes and recipients of thousands of pinpricks of insults and homophobic comments. I believe every sermon damning homosexuality from the pulpit can set off a hate crime if the wrong person is listening.

THE EVER-EXPANSIVE SPIRIT OF GOD

Like many parents of homosexual children, I knew that Gabe was gay from a young age. He always marched to the beat of a different drummer. He was creative, artistic, a lover of plants, origami, and decorating Christmas trees. He worked for a local florist while he was in high school and made exquisite flower arrangements without being taught how to do it. He made beautiful cakes and creative artwork. He was also musically talented and played several instruments. Gabe went to his junior and senior prom with two different young ladies, but there wasn't a spark there; it was more like a social duty he felt compelled to fulfill. I knew he was gay, but I never asked him.

While Gabe was in high school, he attended a Bible study that was taught by a young adult who was particularly anti-gay. We discussed the Bible verses that this young adult was expounding upon, and I assured Gabe that I did not believe that homosexuality was a sin. I emphasized that it was one of the many diversities in this world that God created and that literal biblical interpretations were faulty at best.

Around that same time, Gabe got his learner's permit to drive. The state of Maryland required student drivers to document eighty hours of supervised driving with a licensed driver, so he and I had a lot of time in the car to talk. That is when he told me that he was gay. I assured him of our support and love. There wasn't a coming-out drama in our household. For some young people, sadly,

"IN A RELATIONSHIP"

this event is full of painful rejection and even homelessness. Sometimes the person considers suicide and acts upon it.

~

That fall, Gabe went off to Lebanon Valley College in Annville, Pennsylvania, my alma mater, as a biology major. While attending college he joined a LGBTQIA student group known as "Freedom Rings" and he found many supportive friends there. He loved learning and thrived in the small liberal-arts college environment.

Upon graduation, Gabe began a master's degree program at the University of Illinois, Carbondale Campus, in the field of botany. He was offered a teaching assistantship which included full tuition and a stipend to live on as well. After he completed his master's degree in botany, he was hired to work at the Smithsonian Institution in Suitland, Maryland. There he performs DNA sequencing for a variety of plants, some of which are becoming extinct.

Gabe has spent his young adult years living in the Washington, DC, area and participating in church activities, playing in recorder ensemble groups, teaching music theory to children who no longer have music in their public schools, and socializing with quite a few diverse friends. For a time, he lived in an intentional community house with a group of Quakers, and later he rented space from a woman with disabilities, who had a large husky dog. Gabe would walk the dog around the neighborhood every day and help her around the house. Eventually she needed to move, and Gabe then lived in other group apartments with roommates who shared a common kitchen and living room. When he finally moved into his own apartment, it was a great relief for me as some of his previous residences were challenging situations.

⁐

I always wondered why Gabe never had any personal male dating relationships. He told me he dated a guy once, but they did not seem to hit it off. We never talked about dating, and his constellation of friends seemed to be an eclectic group of church people, musicians, and neighbors. That all ended when I got the phone call announcing that he was in a relationship with a guy named Cris.

Cris is the son of Mexican immigrants from Florida. He is younger than Gabe by twelve years and has worked at a furniture factory as a painter. He is the oldest child in a family of seven children. He enjoys writing science fiction books and poetry, and watching horror movies.

Cris came to visit Gabe in Washington in January of 2019 after they had met on the internet the summer before. They posted many Facebook pictures of the two of them touring all the iconic museums and statues of Washington and walking in the snow.. This was Cris' first time to actually see snow. It also happened that there was a government shutdown during that same week and Gabe, being a government employee, suddenly had additional

"IN A RELATIONSHIP"

free time for this whirlwind visit with his new friend. It appeared to be quite romantic and exciting for the two of them.

In the months that followed, they continued to communicate from a distance and finally decided to live together in Washington. Gabe traveled to Florida a few times and visited Cris' family and, although it seemed they were not overjoyed about their son moving so far away from home, they were accepting of his plans.

I asked Cris if I could send a letter to his mother, as he was preparing to move to Washington. I thought it might be helpful to introduce myself, and he said it was OK. With a Spanish dictionary close at hand, I explained to Cris' mother that we were supportive of her son and would be helpful if he needed anything. She and I communicated a few times on Facebook Messenger in Spanish. She is so young and pretty, and I am old enough to be her mother.

That fall Cris moved to Washington and found a job working at a Dunkin Donuts, got a DC photo ID and some basic health insurance and life as a couple began. Gabe and Cris enjoy the cultural life of Washington as well as the many small ethnic restaurants. They attend both Gabe's church (Episcopal) and Cris' church (Latter Day Saints). Later Cris got another job working as a concierge and began attending community college seeking a degree in early childhood education.

Gabe and Cris came to Pennsylvania to visit us for a few days in the fall of that year and we had a good time getting to know this new young person in our life. I felt a huge age and culture gap between us, but we enjoyed our time of talking and eating together. They visited an Amish Farm Museum in Lancaster, which was a unique experience for Cris. Afterwards there was dinner at a Pennsylvania Dutch Smorgasbord, with many kinds of food Cris tried for the first time.

At Thanksgiving, Cris, Gabe, Mary, and I visited with our oldest son, Peter and his wife Alli, at their home in Virginia. Peter had lived in Virginia for over a decade and worked as a psychologist, and Alli was a nurse. During this holiday visit we played cards, took long walks, went to an all-you-can-eat sushi restaurant, watched movies, and talked far into the nights.

Cris surprised us all by explaining that he was a Dreamer. That meant he was born in Mexico and brought to the United States as a young child. His immigration status is known as Deferred Action on Childhood Arrivals (DACA), which was put in place by former President Obama. Cris is not a citizen, nor is he able to progress in the immigration system at this time as the DACA law continues to be debated by law makers.

Cris is legally able to work and go to some colleges, but he must regularly re-apply with the government to keep his DACA status current and pay a hefty fee. The Supreme Court upheld the status of the DACA recipients

"IN A RELATIONSHIP"

in recent rulings, but their future is still hanging in the balance. How terrible if Cris would ever be deported to Mexico, where he has never lived and knows not a soul. Such an action would be cruel and life-threatening. There are close to a million Dreamers in the United States today.

Suddenly, the reality of Dreamers, which had been on the periphery of my life because of a campus ministry at Delaware State University that I had visited, had now become up-close-and-personal. Cris is my son's beloved, and he became my beloved too. Like transgender people and gay people and people with disabilities, undocumented people should be supported and accepted in this world. We live in a deeply polarized country concerning many issues, and immigration is one of the most challenging. If Cris and Gabe marry eventually, it does not automatically give Cris a quick pathway to citizenship. It is not as easy as it was years ago in the United States. We hold Gabe and Cris in prayer as they journey on in their relationship. My circle of diversity inclusion continues to become wider and deeper.

18

"SPECIAL SESSION OF GENERAL CONFERENCE 2019"

The long-awaited Special Session of General Conference was held February 23-26, 2019. A group of 833 United Methodist delegates (half lay and half clergy) from all over the globe gathered in St. Louis, Missouri, for this four-day conference that was to decide, once-and-for-all, what we would do about homosexuality in our denomination.

The Special Session was held in half of a Convention Center that formerly had been a professional football stadium, and this gave it a subtle flavor of a competition from the very beginning. The other half of the former stadium was rented to a national youth volleyball league that same week. The young people dressed in their athletic shorts and tank-tops in the sub-freezing temperatures

"SPECIAL SESSION OF GENERAL CONFERENCE 2019"

gave an unusual juxtaposition to our international, predominantly older group of United Methodists.

Each day the faithful United Methodists trudged to the convention center from their hotel rooms, and they were greeted with protest groups standing near the front doors, who were present because of the topic of this meeting. Most notable were the folks from the ultra-conservative Westboro Baptist Church who had no lack of signs proclaiming, "gay people are going to hell" and "God hates fags." Pro-LGBTQIA groups, clad in rainbow attire were also standing near them with their signs and banners. I kept my head down and walked swiftly to the designated entrance for the bishops.

The conference began with a day of prayer, worship, and mission-sharing from across the world. It could not have gone any better. The worship was well-crafted with international music, prayers, Scripture reading and soulful testimony about what God was doing through the love and support of the United Methodist Church.

I was a part of the prayer team that helped design this day and had the honor of leading the opening Prayer of Confession. The prayer was written by my transgender spouse, Mary, who used chapter thirteen of the Apostle Paul's first letter to the Corinthians (the "love" chapter) as a basis for the prayer. We confessed that we were not patient or kind or willing to "bear all things, believe all things, hope all things, and endure all things."

We prayed in small groups, we prayed corporately, we fasted, we viewed compelling pictures of our global disaster sites, we anointed each other with oil, and we shared Holy Communion. It appeared that the delegates were of one accord! My hopes were high. It is amazing and puzzling how people can say all the right things about inclusivity, love, unity in a worship setting and yet cannot put it into action when the service ends.

The following day we began the legislation process. The delegates elected a legislative chair, were briefed on Parliamentary Procedures, and trained on how to use the electronic voting pads. The bishops who were presiding also had training before the conference and each presider had a team of three bishops for back-up support. They could not have been more prepared.

The delegates then prioritized the order in which petitions would be handled. The main goal was to choose one of the plans for the church's way forward by the end of this conference. We also were dealing with the issue of how churches could disaffiliate from the denomination for reasons of conscience and a few other items. The members of the thirty-two-member Commission for the Way Forward, those who crafted the three proposed plans (Traditional, One Church, and Connectional Church),

"SPECIAL SESSION OF GENERAL CONFERENCE 2019"

had an opportunity to present before the voting began. It was obvious that this group of incredibly diverse people from every perspective about homosexuality, as well as their age, gender, ethnicity, and orientation had managed to create a bond of trust and unity. The Commission was given a standing ovation at the end of their presentation.

One of the members of the Commission was a professor at Africa University. United Methodist Deaf visitors, seated in the concourse level above the plenary floor where the delegates were seated, began texting me, asking that I arrange an audience with this teacher. They wanted to personally advocate for a Deaf pastor from Ghana, who was applying to become a student at this United Methodist university in Zimbabwe. I was sitting on the stage along with all the other bishops, getting these rapid-fire text messages from the Deaf folks and wondering how I could possibly pull this off.

As the Commission members exited the stage, I jumped up and chased the professor down to the side of the plenary floor and explained who I was and what the Deaf people wanted and pointed to them smiling down at her from the concourse railing above. I voiced what they were signing and signed to them what she was saying and at that moment a meeting was arranged for later in the afternoon. That ultimately led to the admission of the first Deaf student in the history of Africa University. It was for me the only bright moment at this General Conference.

THE EVER-EXPANSIVE SPIRIT OF GOD

The days wore on and it was ultimately decided that the conservative Traditional Plan was the will of the body. It passed by only fifty-four votes, however, so the house was obviously not of one mind. The One Church Plan, (the more centrist approach) was brought forward as a minority report. Although it was presented in a compelling way, it failed to overturn the block of votes that supported the Traditional Plan.

The Traditional Plan kept the conservative language and prohibitions against gay pastors and gay weddings that were already in the *Book of Discipline,* and it added enforcements that mandated compliance in a more punitive way. A person found guilty of breaking the *Book of Discipline* laws about homosexuality (i.e., performing a same gender wedding) at a church trial would have an immediate suspension of employment and benefits for one year as a mandatory sentence. If that pastor had a second violation, they would be immediately defrocked. It also explicitly stated that Boards of Ordained Ministry and bishops could not credential gay people and gave a detailed explanation of what it means to be a "self-avowed and practicing" homosexual. Due process in future church trials was also tightened to avoid any easy dismissal of charges.

"SPECIAL SESSION OF GENERAL CONFERENCE 2019"

Next, we considered the disaffiliation petitions that would allow churches to leave the denomination by paying various fees and obtaining votes from the church members (2/3) and the Annual Conference (a simple majority). This was a significant moment because to allow this was to change our traditional trust clause, which since the beginning of Methodism has stated that assets of a church must revert to the mother denomination when a local church wishes to leave. It was established by our founding father, John Wesley, in the 1700s and was meant to keep in trust the memory and faith of those who first established a particular church and to prevent local congregations from having undue sway over its pastors.

One of the three disaffiliation petitions passed by a razor thin majority of two votes, and it would be in effect immediately in the United States only. The Traditional Plan and all its various enforcements would become law on January 1, 2020, in the United States and twelve months after General Conference 2020 for Annual Conferences in other countries.

During this session of General Conference, the process of conducting business by Parliamentary procedure was chaotic. Roberts Rules of Order are not used in many of the international (Central Conferences), and with forty-two percent of the delegates coming from outside of the United States this way of making decisions, with its many options for questions, points of order, and amendments, was challenging and confusing.

There was translation into ten international languages and American Sign Language simultaneously. With the time lag and the language-nuance issues that comes with translation, it was obvious from some of the questions from the floor that often delegates did not fully understand what was being said. I wonder if the majority rules aspect of Roberts Rules of Order can truly be the way to live together as people of faith. By its very nature it creates winners and losers.

With the passage of the Traditional Plan and the Disaffiliation Petition, the visitors seated on the concourse level above, who were donning rainbow stoles and waving colorful flags and banners, became more and more agitated. Singing and shouting increasingly erupted. Songs like *Jesus Loves Me* could be heard loudly as the presiding bishop continued to handle business acting as if nothing was going on. No calls for order were able to silence this unhappy contingent.

During breaks, I would make my way to the plenary floor where the delegates sat. The Annual Conference delegations sat together in round tables. The Eastern Pennsylvania and Peninsula-Delaware delegates were near one another. The atmosphere was tense as my conferences had delegates who were either progressive or

"SPECIAL SESSION OF GENERAL CONFERENCE 2019"

conservative. People were being hurt and people were hurting one another sometimes by comments said and sometimes on Facebook posts.

By the end of the conference, there were loud and large demonstrations led by grief-stricken progressive folks. Some were arrested as they attempted to break through security and take the floor. There were progressive delegates who were seated on the plenary floor, and they used their right to speak as delegates to make compelling speeches. Groups of them would crowd around a microphone in prayerful support as one of them would testify.

By the last hour of General Conference, things were totally out of control. There was supposed to be a closing worship, but it was scrapped because time ran out and it appeared it would have been undone by protests, tears, and disruption. The president of the Council of Bishops dismissed us with a blessing and with that, the entire meeting was over.

⁓

Within minutes of the end of the conference, the convention center clean-up crew moved in to take down the tables and chairs and to set up what would come in the next day: a monster-truck competition. A couple million tons of topsoil was to be poured onto this very floor where we had been sitting so that trucks with huge wheels could compete for prizes. There was rich symbolism here: All the work done here was soon to be covered over by tons of dirt. Life was moving on at the convention center but our hopes and dreams of a new day, a more open-minded way of life in our denomination seemed hopelessly buried.

The morning we were to fly home from St. Louis, there was freezing rain clinking on the windows of the cab that drove us to the airport. All was dark and freezing cold. As we flew over the iconic arches of St. Louis, I recalled the history of this city. Civil rights for freed slaves and voting rights for women were argued and lost in the very courthouse near where the arches would later be built. Many years later, when these same issues were revisited, slaves were finally given their freedom and women were allowed to vote. Perhaps the history of St. Louis was speaking to me on that icy February morning. *This battle isn't over*, I thought. *The ever-expansive Spirit of God was still at work.*

19

"AFTERMATH"

On the last day of General Conference 2019, when the Traditional Plan with all its enforcements had passed, I wrote to my centrist and progressive pastors and told them I would be available to meet with their churches individually and help their people process what had just happened. I expressed my concern over the hurt and grief they were experiencing and promised I would continue to respect and work with them.

I wrote blogs and e-blasts and set up district-wide listening sessions in which I explained what happened at General Conference, what that meant for the churches, and what was yet to be decided. The disaffiliation petition that had prevailed was in effect immediately after General Conference. Surprisingly, I had no churches come forward asking to disaffiliate at first. A few requests for information trickled in later, but nothing substantial.

THE EVER-EXPANSIVE SPIRIT OF GOD

I spent the next few months visiting districts, churches and talking with individuals about the new General Conference legislation. People came in large numbers to my gatherings, even some newspaper reporters. I showed a PowerPoint presentation at some, had small group conversations with others, and met with individuals as well. One gay pastor who came to my office cried so hard that his tears dropped on the hard-wood conference table, and I could not wipe them away for quite a while. It was a reminder to me of the deep sorrow in the hearts of the people who had longed for some affirmation and new openness in a church that they loved and had faithfully served.

People with more traditional views also found this time to be unsettling, and they were calling even more for a complete split in the denomination and an end to this turmoil. Time for talking was over in their minds. The Wesleyan Covenant Association (WCA), a traditionalist caucus began to strongly advocate for a separation. Several the churches in my areas signed up to become WCA affiliates. Some of these were the largest and wealthiest churches in the area. The WCA held a regional gathering on May 11, 2019, at one of these churches in the Eastern Pennsylvania Conference, so I invited myself to come and give greetings.

In that room were some of the finest pastors and lay people I have grown to love through the years. I gave greetings and reminded them about the importance of the unity of the church. I listened to the keynote address by the group's leader, and it was solidly Wesleyan, hopeful, and not at all mean-spirited. I could not imagine how our church could be the full body of Christ without the distinctive voice of these evangelical members. We needed each other. Why couldn't the two sides understand that? Why could we not simply minister respectfully in our own contexts?

This was the same day that a group of progressive pastors in the Peninsula-Delaware Conference gathered for a big meeting. The leadership of this group would not allow me to visit them, concerned that I might see who was in attendance, as if I did not know who they were! Some also voiced the concern that I had not been a strong-enough advocate for them. I sent a letter of greeting to be read. Being a bishop meant disappointing everyone it seemed. Both sides wanted my full allegiance and neither side trusted me or each other.

Anxiety was deep in the system locally and across the connection. By the summer of 2019, I had spoken at thirty-two events and heard just about every possible opinion and strategy imaginable concerning this dilemma. More importantly, I fielded a lot of pain and grief in a pastoral way. Church went on as always, and surprisingly few congregations withheld apportionment funds from the conference or denomination in protest.

The sessions of Annual Conference in the spring of 2019 were also a source of sadness and tension. This was the year to elect delegates to the 2020 General Conference that would be held in Minneapolis, and the stakes were very high. Everyone wanted to be sure that their people were elected. At the Eastern Pennsylvania Annual Conference many came in rainbow stoles and colorful garments and sang outside of the ordination service. Others crowded at microphones during debates in prayerful support of their speakers. There were unhappy debates about disqualifying nominees for delegation seats. At the end of the day, the Eastern Pennsylvania delegation tally was almost all progressive people. The Peninsula-Delaware delegation was an even 50-50 split.

Afterwards, several conservative pastors and lay people wrote letters and visited my office asking for apologies for how badly they had been treated at the Annual Conference sessions by progressive members. They also were calling for new rules about Annual Conference deportment, and they expressed disappointment that I had not kept order at the conferences.

Across the country, large gatherings of progressive groups began to organize to propose changes in the *Book of Discipline* at the 2020 General Conference. The silent middle/centrists in the United States began to tilt toward the progressives, feeling that the enforcements of the Traditional Plan had gone too far. A group known as "UMC Next," met at the Church of the Resurrection UMC in Leewood, Kansas, to strategize ways to allow the LGBTQIA community into full inclusion in the church.

Another group known as "UMC Forward," included many other issues such as the eradication of racism, classism, sexism, colonialism, white privilege and, of course, heterosexism. They gathered in Minneapolis, Minnesota, and proposed that the denomination dissolve and divide itself into four branches.

A group of United Methodists from Africa, Europe, and the Philippines called for regional connections as a way of solving our dilemma in a legislative proposal known as the "Christmas Covenant." This would maintain unity by allowing various regions to handle homosexuality in their local context.

One of the African bishops began yet another think-tank gathering, which much later presented a document known as "The Protocol."

The Western Jurisdiction affirmed their stand on breaking the discriminatory rules of the *Book of Discipline* and offered themselves as a place of sanctuary for pastors who felt they were unsafe in their home conference due to their sexual orientation or theological positions. I even sent them a pastor from my area who was seeking such relief.

THE EVER-EXPANSIVE SPIRIT OF GOD

⁓

The traditional side of the Methodist house was also hard at work, and the various caucus groups that made up this body devised legislation known as "The Indianapolis Plan." It would essentially divide the denomination and its assets and allow churches and conferences to go their separate ways.

In the fall, I visited districts in both of my conferences and presented these many options. I also included a teaching about community outreach and stressed that this battle over homosexuality was not the main thing we do as Christians. Being the tangible "love of Christ" in the world was the mission of the church, I insisted, and no matter how we voted at General Conference in 2020 the United Methodist Church should still have a story of love, grace, and salvation to proclaim in Word and in deed.

⁓

Still, there were plenty of people at these district events who just wanted to debate homosexuality. But I always believed that this battle about homosexuality was never about homosexuality. It felt as if the LGBTQIA community was being used as a scapegoat for the real issues, which were more about power and a perceived loss of power by groups and individuals who had always held sway over the decision-making and leadership preferences in the church, which sway had been slowly eroding for the last fifty years in favor of more diversity, openness, and inclusivity.

Dividing the church was a simple and destructive answer to an extremely complex problem. It was never about the Bible's six verses against homosexuality. It was never about some iron-clad promise made at someone's ordination to follow the *Book of Discipline*. The real conversation for the future is how we can and should be the presence of Christ in this world.

20

"TEAR DOWN THE WALL"

In November of 2019, the Council of Bishops met at the Lake Junaluska Retreat Center in North Carolina for their fall meeting. This would be our last meeting before our gathering in Minneapolis for General Conference 2020. We had conversation about the Judicial Council rulings that we had requested about the constitutionality of the enforcements of the Traditional Plan and about four delegates who voted at the General Conference who apparently were not properly credentialed. Since the disaffiliation petition passed by only two votes there was hope that this legislation would be deemed out of order because we did not know which side the uncredentialed delegates supported. In both cases the Judicial Council gave disappointing rulings for the progressive side. The enforcements stayed in place as written and would go in

"TEAR DOWN THE WALL"

effect on January 1, 2020, and the disaffiliation petition remained legal.

At this meeting, we elected new officers, participated in a deeply convicting workshop on racism and colonialism, and engaged in well-crafted worship experiences and fervent prayer. Despite all its complexity and tension, it was a profound honor and privilege to sit in that room. I usually said very little, but I was always fully engaged and wrote copious notes to absorb the depth of the process. Sometimes I played the piano for the worship services.

The most moving and heart-changing presentation for me at this Council of Bishops meeting was a worship service led by our bishops from Germany at an open session. They shared about the 30th anniversary of the fall of the Berlin Wall in 1989. It had divided East and West Germany since the end of World War II. The wall had been a grim reminder of the deep divide between Western Democracy and Eastern Communism and symbolized the Cold War era that affected much of Europe for decades.

For years, families were physically separated from one another and numerous people attempting to cross over the wall had been shot and killed by the East German border guards. The destruction of this formidable barrier was clearly a movement of the Holy Spirit. Someone in Germany at the time said, "The Communist government was no match for prayer and candles." (Candlelight vigils had been a big part of the movement that ultimately reunified this country and, miraculously, on that night when the wall came down not a shot had been fired. I sat glued to my seat as the bishops from Germany shared their personal stories.

My colleagues who led the worship did not miss the chance to compare the deeply divided Germany with the United Methodist Church and its long-standing impasse over homosexuality. They reminded us of the passage in Ephesians 2:14, which proclaims "For [Jesus] himself is our peace, who has made the two groups one and has destroyed the barrier, the dividing wall of hostility." During that service, I realized that the time had come for the church to tear down this wall of controversy.

We sang a hymn that was written during this amazing time in German history. Even though we sang an English translation of this historic song, the message was clear: "Have faith in God's new pathways, walk on in this new day."

I came home from the Council of Bishops meeting convinced that the church was on a Berlin Wall journey and that I could not in good conscience execute the enforcements of the Traditional Plan when they became law on January 1, 2020. I wrote a pastoral letter to my conferences explaining about the importance of the entire body of Christ being included in our church that said in part:

Catch sight of God's vision of a church that is busy making disciples of Jesus Christ, a church that is engaging in ministry and mission, a church striving for equality and equity for all people. We can only get there as we employ with grace all the giftedness of the Body of Christ, not just one side or the other. Dividing our church would cut off some of our needed giftedness. We can only accomplish this vibrant ministry as we tear down the walls in our hearts and, "Do justice, love mercy and walk humbly with our God" (Micah 6:8).

I included in this pastoral letter a declaration that I would never again refer homosexuality complaints to church trial:

As your bishop, I am bound to receive and process complaints, but I do not believe it is helpful to engage in church trials. So, I will not refer any such complaints for a church trial. I say this not out of a sense of rebellion against the rules in our *Book of Discipline* but out of my pastor's heart that wishes to defend the people of our conferences against this destructive, divisive, and expensive process.

This letter was what the progressive side of the house had been hoping I would write. Their response was a wave of appreciation from many, but I heard very little from the most liberal leaders in the conference. It took a week or so, but the traditional folks began to speak out strongly with disapproval and disappointment.

The previous session of Annual Conference in Eastern Pennsylvania, with its protest-like show of rainbow stoles and majority-elected progressive delegates was still fresh in people's minds. Now I was clearly siding with the progressives, refusing to obey the words of the *Book of Discipline*, which I had vowed to uphold at my consecration as bishop.

There were not a few calls for my resignation and a request for information about how to file a complaint against me for breaking my vows. I had clearly burned any centrist bridge I had tried to build, and it was both an unsettling time and one of personal liberation. I had publicly refused to participate in a church trial ever again. I had torn down that wall, at least for me. I believed that homosexual people need to be defended, and not demonized by the church's new enforcements.

If I were to be found guilty of not keeping my consecration vows, it would be OK with me. No complaint ever came, but attendance at most of my meetings with pastors and laity dropped off considerably. My cabinets and staff were not disapproving or approving for the most part, and we just moved on with the considerable work of preparing for General Conference 2020 and making clergy appointments that spring.

"TEAR DOWN THE WALL"

It was a lonely time for me, to be sure. In general, the position of bishop is isolating in many ways, and admitting when your heart is breaking is not something one should do publicly or with colleagues. I thank God for my beloved spouse, my Mary, who was my greatest support and strength throughout this entire journey.

21

"THE PROTOCOL"

Christmas of 2019 was a little sad for me. I was completing twelve years of service as the bishop of the Philadelphia area, and the *Book of Discipline* clearly states that bishops can serve no more than twelve years in any one area. Knowing that I would be moving in the summer after Jurisdictional Conference made this holiday season my last time to do those things at Christmastime that had become a precious tradition to me. These included Christmas dinners with the cabinet and staff, the holiday district service projects, and the Christmas Eve Candlelight service at the historic Barratts Chapel in Frederica, Delaware.

On Christmas Day, Mary and I volunteered at an early morning feeding program for people without housing in inner city Philadelphia. How I loved this particular church and its heart for economic justice and equality for the LGBTQIA community. Mary and I also visited the

"THE PROTOCOL"

home of one of the other city pastors for a housewarming celebration that same day, amid much joy and laughter.

The week after Christmas was quiet. I took time to prepare for my cabinet retreats. Mary and I took long walks along the canal and tried to imagine what life would be like a year from then. On New Year's Eve, I went to bed at my normal time. I never stay up until midnight, but the gunshots and firecrackers from the neighbors always wake me up when the New Year arrives. After the noise had died down that night, I laid in bed wondering what would happen to our denomination at General Conference 2020. One thing I knew for sure was that we would not be in this house when the clock struck midnight the following year.

On New Year's Day, an email came from the president of the Council of Bishops instructing all the bishops to be on a conference call on January 2, 2020, for an emergency meeting. A small group of sixteen leaders of the church had come up with a plan for the denomination's orderly separation, and they wanted to tell us what it was all about before it became public on January 3. Leading this think-tank group was a bishop from Sierra Leone, Bishop John Yambasu, and it included leaders of all the movements around the connection: traditional, progressive, centrist, American, and international. They called their plan, "The Protocol."

On the January 2 phone call, we learned that a professional mediator had agreed to process this conversation, which had involved many face-to-face meetings throughout the summer and fall. This mediator was from a prominent law firm and was of the Jewish faith, so he had no skin in the game of the potential schism. However, he was a highly skilled professional who was intrigued by our dilemma and had volunteered to lead the process.

The phone conversation that day included an overview of The Protocol that the group of sixteen had crafted. I was grateful for the heads-up, but we all felt a little shocked at both the secrecy and the enormity of this plan. It would involve a recognition that we as a denomination were now at a place where we needed to bless one another and go our separate ways at the May 2020 General Conference. The Protocol included a process for how traditional churches and even entire traditional annual conferences could leave the United Methodist denomination with their properties and assets and form a new denomination. This exiting expression of Methodism would receive $25 million dollars (over several years) from the existing denomination's coffers.

There were provisions for an additional $39 million dollars for ethnic churches and ministries over time during this transition. The plan also included an additional $2 million dollars to be set aside for any other group, perhaps a progressive body, of at least 100 churches, that also wanted to break off and start something new.

"THE PROTOCOL"

Individual churches and entire Annual Conferences could vote to leave with a mere 57% majority. If a particular conference voted to leave the denomination and be a part of this new conservative movement, the churches in that conference that wanted to remain with the United Methodist Church could affiliate with another Annual Conference across the Methodist connection.

With the optimism of believing that we could finally find peace at the 2020 General Conference, I looked forward to the announcement of The Protocol on January 3. But when it was made public, the secular news outlets picked it up and proclaimed that it was a done deal and that the United Methodist Church, the second largest mainline Protestant denomination in the United States, had already split! My phone voice mail and email in-box immediately filled with requests for interviews by local newspapers and TV stations.

I quickly sent out a letter to the churches stating that a schism had not been decided, we had to wait until General Conference and that, even then, it might not happen. We needed to remain calm and to pray, I said. It was hard to convince people of this, however, when the prominent news outlets were already proclaiming schism. People also did not always read my statements, and I had to keep repeating the same message for several weeks.

THE EVER-EXPANSIVE SPIRIT OF GOD

In the months that followed, the makers of several other proposals that were set to go to General Conference regarding a possible new form of unity were beginning to say that they would prefer to only deal with The Protocol. General Conference was a ten-day event, and logistically it would be impossible to deal with all the other plans and leave Minneapolis with any concrete decisions. Most of us felt it was finally time to call it a day as a unified body. The 2019 General Conference had not accomplished much except to teach the church that legalistic enforcements could not and would not create unity or peace.

In addition to The Protocol's arrival in the New Year, there was also a communication from the headquarters of Reconciling Ministry Network (the progressive caucus that promoted full inclusion of the LGBTQIA community) to their member churches and conferences. This letter reminded folks that the enforcements directives of the 2019 General Conference had gone into effect on January 1, 2020. These new enforcements would ramp up penalties for pastors who performed gay weddings and bishops who ordained or commissioned gay pastors, and it gave far-reaching avenues in which to determine if a person was gay, to prevent them from entering ministry.

The Reconciling Ministry Network (RMN) encouraged their units to go to their respective bishops and urge them to suspend all church trials and complaints against people who broke the homosexuality rules. Since I had

"THE PROTOCOL"

already announced my position to suspend all trials that pertained to homosexuality back in the fall, the RMN in my conferences were encouraged to write bishops like me letters of support and to arrange for a meeting with them.

The Reconciling Ministry Network committee from the Peninsula-Delaware Conference soon came to the Annual Conference center in Dover, Delaware, on a cold January evening and presented me a large packet of thank-you letters and a beautiful woven rainbow scarf. We shared Holy Communion together, and I thanked them for this outpouring of support.

Most touching to me that night were gay and lesbian people who spoke candidly about how an affirming local United Methodist Church in Delaware had given them hope and self-esteem. Many other churches they had visited in the past had denounced homosexuality openly from the pulpit. I thought, *What an amazing outreach opportunity we would have if we would become affirming of everyone.*

I waited a long time to hear from the Reconciling Ministry Network Committee of the Eastern Pennsylvania Conference, but eventually the group met with me at the Annual Conference center. We shared in conversation and Holy Communion. My spouse, Mary, wrote a special communion liturgy for the service we had that night.

THE EVER-EXPANSIVE SPIRIT OF GOD

I eagerly wanted to talk with the RMN because of their strong showing at Annual Conference the prior year, winning most of the delegate-seat elections and creating a colorful stir with their rainbow stoles, spirited singing before the ordination service, and crowding at the microphones during hot debates.

I explained about the pain and anger that many conservative folks had expressed to me about their deportment. They were especially hurt about the motion to disqualify conservative young adults running for election as delegates simply because they had a part in worship or at the plenary session. This call to disqualify the conservative young people did not prevail, but the discussion had been very painful.

I reminded them that the 2020 Annual Conference would be so crucial for the future of our church and asked them directly if they wanted to drive out the centrists who were somewhat on the fence about all of this with another show of overt force. Their answer was yes, they intended to keep the pressure on. They felt this was the way they had successfully pursued justice and nothing could stop them from following that call.

I suppose that is how any justice movement is ever accomplished in this world. Abolition, women's suffrage, women's liberation, any number of human rights victories are hard-fought and won through strong protests, beatings, and sometimes death. Racism, sexism, homophobia is not easily overturned, and I respect the courage of those who took the hard stands in the past and fought for

"THE PROTOCOL"

human rights. It puts me in a difficult spot, however, as a bishop who is called to preserve the unity of the church.

Yet I think back to a time when I thought that gay people were sinners and I interpreted the Bible much more literally than I do now. I was not won over by marches, protests, or voting at large assembly meetings. It happened because of quiet conversations with gay people with hearts as big as the sun, who melted the ice of my preconceived ideas and helped me to see humanity in a better way.

Perhaps we need both approaches, and my yearning for a theologically diverse church was never likely to come through quiet diplomacy. It didn't matter now. We were heading to Minneapolis and the denomination would be broken in two when The Protocol passed.

But God had other plans for the world in 2020.

22

"COVID-19"

While the conversation about The Protocol continued to crescendo, there was an outbreak of a strange and deadly new virus in Wuhan, China. This virus was a highly contagious flu, there was no cure or vaccine, and it began spreading rapidly around the world. People were dying in great numbers, and it especially affected seniors and people with pre-existing health conditions. News reports showed people on the streets in China wearing masks, and eventually the government there forced everyone to stay sequestered in their homes to limit social contact.

Although I felt sad for China, I wasn't much concerned. I could remember a time when there was a virus known as SARS in 2003. A few years after that there was The Swine Flu (N1H1) and we all got flu shots for that. The thought of this coronavirus, called Covid-19 because it was first recognized in 2019, coming to the United

"COVID-19"

States and creating havoc like we had never seen did not cross my mind. But soon the virus arrived.

~

It hit hard at first in Washington State and California early in 2020. We prayed earnestly for the people there, but life went on as usual in the rest of the country and in my churches. We had the annual Youth Rally in January with nearly 3,000 teenagers in a large Ocean City Convention Center, and we held many other conference events and workshops in January and February. We would soon learn to be fearful of meeting face to face, even at church services.

There was a major meeting of traditional United Methodist leaders from around the world on March 2-4, 2020, in Atlanta, Georgia. They drafted a formal proposal for a "New Methodist Movement" for a global church in preparation for the expected schism at General Conference 2020. It outlined a new denomination's mission, doctrine, and structure. The manifesto was signed by all the known leaders of the conservative United Methodist caucus groups and a few United Methodist bishops. There were twenty-eight signatures in all, twenty-four men and four women; almost all of them were white people.

Like The Protocol statement of January 3, the New Methodist Movement document hit like a sudden lightning strike, and it signaled that the division of the UMC was moving forward. No turning back. Then within days, without much warning, the virus struck. There is a saying that "Life is what happens when we humans are making plans," and it certainly did then.

⁓

During the first week of March, the governors of the states most affected began to raise stronger voices than the national governmental leadership. More and more states were reporting frightening numbers of COVID-19 cases and deaths. New York, New Jersey, and parts of Pennsylvania were beginning to see major increases of cases in their hospitals, and ICU beds became scarce. By the second week of March, the governors were calling for limits on the number of people gathering in any one room.

Large sporting events were canceled, no basketball March Madness, the theatres in New York City were shuttered, and eventually the 2020 Summer Olympics in Tokyo were called off. I began writing pastoral letters telling people they should not hold worship services if there were more than fifty people in a room. This was not a problem for many of our churches, because most had far less than fifty people in attendance at any one service. Then the governors of the states began to say that no more than ten people could gather in a room. and that was the end of all worship services.

"COVID-19"

In a series of increasingly dire pastoral letters, I called for our churches to stop meeting in person altogether and, although I got some push-back at first, the news media silenced most of the protests with the horror of staggering death statistics and video footage of people on breathing machines in intensive care units. The refrigerator trucks in the parking lots of many hospitals to take away the bodies of the dead sent a chilling message that this was an unprecedented catastrophe. There were not enough testing kits, ICU ventilators, or face masks and our nation was grossly unprepared for this pandemic.

Medical ships that were usually sent abroad to poverty-stricken countries were being deployed to affected areas in our country. Hotels, campus sports arenas, even churches were becoming staging areas for medical exams and hospital wards. Some vacationers were stranded on cruise ships that were full of infected people and not allowed to dock at any port. When passengers were finally allowed to disembark, they were rushed to military bases for fourteen days of quarantine.

Nursing homes and senior living facilities were especially hard hit. They were reporting the rapid spread of cases and many deaths among residents and staff. National Guard troops were called out to some major cities to distribute food and essential supplies and even take over some overwhelmed nursing homes. Eventually all public schools and colleges were closed for the rest of the year. Some schools were able to continue instruction online,

THE EVER-EXPANSIVE SPIRIT OF GOD

but those without the luxury of computers or Internet access at home had no options. Teachers had to grapple with a whole new way of teaching and keeping order on a computer screen. For many students, free breakfast and lunch programs that the schools provided were their main source of nutrition; and parents were scrambling for other options. Graduating high school seniors did not have their proms or graduation ceremonies.

⁓

Everyone was beginning to know someone who was sick or dying or dead. Funerals and weddings also had to be postponed or held with only a small number present, usually outdoors and with social distancing. Families (and clergy) were not allowed to visit nursing homes, or even the hospitals where loved ones lay dying. Employees at medical facilities were working long hours and were exhausted, getting sick, or quitting. Toilet paper and hand sanitizer flew off the shelves in every grocery store.

Every part of life had suddenly changed, and I was writing sympathy letters every day to people who had lost a loved one. I also sent out copious letters of encouragement and instructions to the churches about how to continue ministry in these times. Pastors were overwhelmed and exhausted.

The conferences I served encompassed three states: Pennsylvania, Delaware, and Maryland. Each governor had something different to say as time passed, and it was challenging to keep it all straight. One state ordered a 14-day quarantine for anyone who came into their borders. Another required face masks all the time, others said only when inside public places. One governor even had different rules for different parts of the state.

Many stores and other businesses were shuttered, and that stopped a great deal of money from flowing into peoples' pockets. People of color were affected the most, and low-income or unemployed people were literally without food or rent money for their landlords because they were out of work. Testing for the virus was also extremely limited, and the communities who had the most cases of the disease were often without the testing and health services they needed.

Our churches and pastors mobilized and did what they could to help. They fed school children and raised money for people who were out of work. Worship services were conducted on YouTube, Zoom, Facebook live streaming platforms, or even by conference call. Our pastors engaged in meaningful and creative Bible studies and sermons during this very strange season of Lent 2020.

When Holy Week and Easter rolled around, it was yet another sad reminder that normal life was on hold. Our faithful pastors and laity found ways of proclaiming the death and resurrection of Christ with video footage, drive-in services in a parking lot with a bullhorn, and doorstep Easter lily and palm branch deliveries. We also began virtually consecrating communion elements (bread and grape juice in the Methodist tradition). As this pandemic dragged on, people needed the comfort and presence of Holy Communion more than ever.

We also learned that church meetings could go on with a Zoom video conferencing program, usually quite efficiently. Meetings that often took hours were accomplished in a much shorter amount of time, and no one had to leave their house. People were watching video services online who had never attended church before, and Deaf people were participating in virtual services around the country in American Sign Language in great numbers.

During the chaos of all the closures and stay-at-home orders, major convention centers were also canceling their venues. The Minneapolis Convention Center let the Commission on General Conference know that they would not be able to hold our UM General Conference 2020 in May. The Jurisdictional Conference slated for July 2020 also had to be postponed, because by rule it can only happen eight weeks after a session of General Conference. Eventually, we all had to postpone our June Annual Conference sessions to the fall as well. Our usual way of conducting business as a denomination was washed away like a sandcastle hit by an ocean wave.

The workload also came in waves. First came all the letters telling people to stop meeting, then telling people to apply for government subsidies for payroll protections,

"COVID-19"

then the Holy Week flurry of on-line services and activities. I produced numerous video sermons for the website and recorded personal greetings and devotional talks using only my smartphone camera. Then there was the tedious rescheduling dismantling the entire agenda of spring banquets, meetings, and special events. I never worked so hard in all my life, but I didn't drive a single mile in my car.

The Annual Conference leaders, staff, district superintendents, and I made appointments of pastors to their assignments that would begin in July using video conference calls. My spouse, Mary, was serving as an interim pastor at the time at a congregation nearby, and I became the camera crew for her video sermons on Sunday mornings!

Suddenly there was an eerie (but very welcomed) silence around our denominational schism, The Protocol, and the New Global Methodist Movement. Not a peep from anyone about homosexuality. It appeared we would all have to be together as the United Methodist Church a while longer. We were in a strange and wondrous forced respite, with no light at the end of the tunnel.

I would be staying in my current episcopal assignment past the twelve-year limit. Bishops cannot move apart from a session of Jurisdictional Conference and that could not happen as scheduled. All my expectations about packing and moving in September, all my wistful this-is-my-last-Christmas thoughts of the year before, suddenly were off the table because of this virus.

The air outdoors was never cleaner or the sky bluer than it was during the spring of 2020, as the pandemic raged on and fewer people were in cars polluting the air. I prayed that our spiritual air would follow suit.

23

"PANDEMIC OF RACISM"

The spring of 2020 also saw a perfect storm for racial unrest in the United States. The COVID-19 pandemic was affecting people of color at an extraordinarily high rate. Poverty, employment in high-risk-for-virus-exposure settings, low paying jobs, lay-offs, educational and childcare disruption, public transportation cutbacks, cramped living environments, poor and/or uninsured health-care treatment options all created additional risk of sickness and death for them from this dangerous virus. Institutional racism was at the heart of it all. Since its inception, the United States has been hard-wired for white supremacy and the subjugation and abuse of people of color in order to garner wealth and power. Some United Methodists have always known this and strove to fight to correct it, including supporting the Abolitionist movement, but the UMC was also guilty of systematic institutional racism.

Racism had been going on in the United States for more than 400 years. Most people, like myself, never took a good hard look at it. I grew up in my safe white bubble of middle-class, segregated America. I had served two parishes that had African American members but never saw the obvious inequities as a cause-and-effect kind of thing. It just "was what it was" in my racist and clueless way of thinking. Nothing was ever taught to me about Black History in school. I never connected that my white privilege was paid for by people of color. Throughout my ministry I missed a million opportunities to work for racial justice, and for that I am and will always be deeply sorry.

When I became a bishop in 2008, I attempted to address some of this. I observed Martin Luther King, Jr.'s birthday and Black History Month with special services and opportunities for service. I engaged in much study, truth-telling, re-allocation of resources, and balancing positions of leadership. I worked on a project to forgive past debts of historically black churches, and apologized for white racism. I worked on Black church-history projects and helped improve cross-racial and cross-cultural appointments of pastors. Every single person entering ministry or leadership in the church in both of my

"PANDEMIC OF RACISM"

Annual Conferences was required to take a three-day racism training course.

All of this was an attempt to correct many of the racist wrongs of the past in the church, but it fell far short of making a difference. It was merely a veneer of saying all the right things many times while discrimination and white supremacy were baked into the system as solid as cement. The realization that we Methodists had a pandemic of racism in 2020 unleashed an urgency in the denomination like I had never seen before.

The spark that set off this explosion-waiting-to-happen was the suffocation death of a black man by a police officer in Minneapolis, Minnesota, in May of 2020. The victim, George Floyd, was being questioned for allegedly passing a counterfeit $20 bill at a neighborhood store. During the arrest, he was thrown to the ground, handcuffed, and one officer pressed his knee on Floyd's neck for over eight minutes. During this horrific scene, bystanders were taking videophone footage in which Mr. Floyd was crying out that he couldn't breathe and calling for his mother, and then he was dead. This was police brutality in broad daylight, with no apparent remorse on the part of the officers involved. And at first, there was very little response from the police department concerning the culpability of those involved.

This incident sparked an immediate national outcry and rage that instantly swept through the entire nation as the video footage of this incident was shown multiple times on virtually every news outlet and was repeated on millions of social media platforms instantly. There were other similar horrific acts of violence against black people around this same time, and video cameras were recording it all. Every major city had weeks of protests, some peaceful, some violent on both sides, including looting, fires, tear gas, and rubber bullets.

The United Methodist Church sprang into action creating several webinars about dismantling racism, setting up many training events to teach people about the deep scourge of systemic racism in this country. We also studied the dark history of our church's segregation and oppression of people of color. I participated in several peaceful protest marches in the streets of the small towns in Delaware and Maryland.

I received quite a few letters complaining that the Black Lives Matter demonstrations were "fascist" and that I had no business supporting it as a bishop. Some members left the United Methodist Church and others threatened that they would withhold their offerings if I didn't stop talking about racism. I answered every letter with quiet determination, insisting that white people needed to take a long look at the facts. People of color have been denigrated by our society for centuries, I said, in a country that proclaims liberty and justice for all.

"PANDEMIC OF RACISM"

I wrote numerous articles and spoke at several webinars and live events that addressed racism. We Methodists were all reading books, attending Juneteenth events, and watching documentaries—breathlessly driven yet sometimes at a loss as to what we could do to make a difference.

The incidences of the coronavirus were slowing down in May of 2020 and the governors across the country were loosening the stay-at-home restrictions. We even began having in-person meetings in our offices with a careful eye to social distancing, mask-wearing, hand-washing, and vigilant cleaning of ventilation systems, bathrooms, desks, and tables. Everything smelled like bleach.

With these loosened restrictions came a series of webinars that gave churches guidance about how to begin worship again safely. Some churches and pastors refused to abide by these safety measures. Some believed this was nothing but "liberal politics" at work and all we needed was faith in God to protect us. Some paid a dear price for living in denial and it cost some churches the lives of its members. Incidences of COVID super-spreader events happened at some of these congregations.

Many churches went back to in-person worship by mid-June. Most of the African American Churches and churches of color did not and continued worship using virtual platforms. They were taking no chances, and I applauded their caution.

Racism was on my front-burner of concern at that time. I was shocked to get an e-mail from one of the LGBTQIA advocates that spring asking why I had not paid attention to the plight of gay people lately. I was stunned. It was true that the LGBTQIA struggle for the heart and soul of the United Methodist Church had been less of a conversation in recent months with the focus on the twin pandemics of COVID and racism. People sometimes were not able to see the intersectionality between justice causes and the need to work for everyone's rights. We couldn't just focus on one marginalized group's agenda to the exclusion of the other, but that kind of conversation is always a challenge as we all care deeply about the things that affect us the most.

24

"ENGAGEMENT"

In the fall of 2020, there was a resurgent second wave of the coronavirus and the number of sick and dying people, which had dropped in the summer. This time large outbreaks began happening in areas in the mountains of Pennsylvania and the upper-Midwest of the United States, which hadn't seen as much of this virus previously. Covid-19 was an equal-opportunity disease, and even more contagious mutations of the virus were already being discovered in Europe, South Africa, and India and quickly coming to the United States.

The response of the United States administration and the state governors was largely uncoordinated, and this added to the spread. Some lawmakers were in denial about the disease and made it an issue that divided people on either side of the political spectrum. Some prominent leaders refused to wear masks and there was demonizing of governors and officials who put controls in place that affected commerce.

In the state of Pennsylvania, the chief health officer was a physician named Dr. Rachel Levine. She appeared on local television and social media often giving health updates and warnings, some of which went unheeded and some were mocked and cursed. That was partly because Dr. Rachel Levine, a prominent pediatrician, was a transgender woman. As I watched her health updates on Facebook-Live, there was much transphobic hate speech being typed into the chat, often with red or angry emoji faces floating up the side of the screen.

One day after Dr. Levine gave her health update, she addressed the transphobic comments. She admonished the people to foster a spirit of acceptance and welcoming to the LBGTQIA community and celebrate the wonderful diversity of the Commonwealth. The nasty, hate-filled comments continued, but I knew in my heart that some young people struggling with their gender identity got a bit more courage because of Dr. Rachel Levine.

The presidential election campaign was in full swing in the fall of 2020, and there was no lack of polarization in the country or the church. Church folks were deeply conflicted about who should win the 2020 election. To add to my anxiety, our son Gabe and his partner Cris decided to take a trip to Florida to visit Cris' family. Florida at the

"ENGAGEMENT"

time was one of the COVID-19 hot spots, with hospitals at capacity and much racial and political tension due to the upcoming election. The last thing I wanted was my son on public transportation (where many refused to wear face masks) and visiting a state that had health care challenges. The two went anyway and took a sleeper-car Amtrak train to Tampa from DC and spent a week there. Cell phone pictures they sent to me from Florida depicted much loving family time with joyous meals and big smiles with Chis' family.

On the last day, a surprising picture dropped into my text message box that announced that Gabe had asked Cris to marry him. He did it by writing on a large stone , "Will you marry me?" (Cris had asked Gabe to make their relationship official by proposing to Gabe after they met in person for the first time in January 2019. The ball had been in Gabe's court to make the next proposal.) Cris has a love of rocks and minerals, and the stone used in this proposal was in reference to the movie *A Bug's Life*. Cris accepted Gabe's written-on-stone marriage proposal, and Cris' family was as supportive as the family members on our side.

Gabe and Cris announced that they would be waiting a few years to get married. I hoped that the immigration issue would improve with a more immigration-friendly future government. I also prayed that the COVID-19 pandemic would end by then and life and travel would go back to normal. Gabe and Cris arrived back in Washington, DC, without any incident, and I was greatly relieved.

THE EVER-EXPANSIVE SPIRIT OF GOD

The re-scheduled Annual Conference sessions held in the fall of 2020 for both Peninsula-Delaware and Eastern Pennsylvania were conducted by Zoom. Voting was handled electronically, and it was slow and tedious. There were many preparatory meetings where we voted "electronic rules of order," which included the limiting of business to only the basics and dispensing with amendments or prolonged debate.

The practical preparations, the numerous versions of the scripts, the confusing voting platform idiosyncrasies, and the large number of frustrated delegates were just a few of the issues that we faced in the weeks leading up to the two separate virtual Annual Conference sessions. The rules for engagement were unlike anything we had ever experienced, and the newness of it all was exhausting. The staff in both conferences worked tirelessly preparing pre-recorded videos, sending out information, arranging for "in person" options, and answering hundreds of questions.

The usual resolutions about homosexuality that had been a part of every Annual Conference session since I had become a bishop were absent that year. What a relief it was to me not to have to deal with unhappy interchanges at microphones, multiple amendments, hurt feelings, and deeply hurt, often crying people on both sides.

Despite none of the usual debates about homosexuality at these virtual sessions, there were still the

"ENGAGEMENT"

"disaffiliation" resolutions at both Annual Conference sessions. In the Eastern Pennsylvania Conference there was one church seeking disaffiliation, and in the Peninsula-Delaware Conference there were four. The Annual Conferences voted to allow all of them to disaffiliate.

2020 was a time of sadness for me, a harbinger of things to come. In my opinion, whenever a local congregation leaves the denomination we are all diminished. The reasons for leaving were fraught with impatience and a belief that if they could just "get away" from the United Methodist Church they would be free to do ministry in their own way. They would be free from the hurtful words in the *Book of Discipline*, paying apportionments, and being assigned a pastor by a bishop. But I felt they would no longer be a part of the bigger ministry of the United Methodist Church that was doing so much good in the world. Our system also provided supervision and clergy quality controls and a safety net of support that I worried they would surely miss when other internal conflicts arose.

I sympathized with those on the progressive side who felt burdened by the *Book of Discipline's* prohibition against the LGBTQIA community and wanted to be open and affirming without fear of reprisal. Yet I would have preferred the progressive churches to stay and work for a better day from within the system.

I grieved as well over the traditionalist who felt a need to leave in such a hurry. The *Book of Discipline* still said what they believed: no gay pastors, no gay weddings. Yet they claimed with certainty that the denomination was moving in a "bad direction" and they could not continue to serve God in any institution that would even consider a live-and-let-live flexibility around the issues of homosexuality. They also blamed me, their bishop, for the need to leave, because I announced that I would not refer anyone to a church trial. Still, I would have preferred they would have stayed as well and work for a better day from within the system.

Both Annual Conferences had in-person ordination and memorial services that year, but they were by invitation only, with a very small number of people present and a good deal of social distancing, face mask wearing, handwashing, and no singing. Between my laying on of hands of each of the ordinands, for example, I washed with hand sanitizer. All of this felt so strange.

Christmas in 2020 came and Mary and I were still living in Pennsylvania. We stayed home during the holidays. There were no cabinet and staff Christmas dinners, and the Advent and Christmas services were all done virtually. I didn't have the heart to decorate the house for Christmas. No one was coming to visit, and I had given our

"ENGAGEMENT"

old fake Christmas tree away the year before because I thought we were moving!

I recorded a sermon for a virtual Christmas Eve service at the historic Barratts Chapel in Frederica, Delaware. I preached about the Christmas carol, *O Little Town of Bethlehem,* which was written by Rev. Phillips Brooks over 150 years ago during the challenging time of the Civil War. Things were polarized and difficult then as now. The words, "The hopes and fears of all the years are met in thee tonight," spoke to my heart like never before during that Christmas season.

There was hope and joy in the midst of it all for our family, however. On December 5, 2020, our first grandchild was born. He is the son of our oldest son, Peter, and his wife, Alli. We would have loved to have traveled to Virginia to see them and welcome baby Colton to the world, but it just wasn't safe or wise as the pandemic continued to escalate. We engaged them on video calls and cherished every picture of the baby they texted to us. God was bringing light and life into the world again, even during the most challenging of years.

25

"DISAFFILIATIONS OF THE HEART"

Life continued under the threat of the COVID-19 pandemic as January 2021 rolled around. After much prayer and conversation with trusted friends, it was clear to me that I needed to submit a request for retirement. The denominational coffers that care for the Episcopal Fund were greatly depleted, income from apportionment dollars were lower than usual due to the pandemic, and there was a need for jurisdictions to consider having fewer bishops. My area, which had two separate small conferences, would be ideal for coupling with larger sister conferences.

I had served as bishop in parts of Pennsylvania, Maryland, and Delaware for thirteen years at that point, and I did not feel called to seek another placement with only a few years left before my mandatory retirement. I was tired of the politics, the workload, and the conflicts. I knew I could engage in some Deaf and disability ministries in retirement, which idea I loved. Also, it was time that my spouse, Mary could finally come out and live openly as her true self. This surely would also give us both an opportunity to engage in transgender ministry.

We purchased a home in Carrollton, Virginia, near our oldest son and his wife and their new baby, and I requested retirement effective September 1, 2021. All this was very un-ceremonial because all in-person meetings of the Annual Conference, Jurisdictional Conference and the Council of Bishops had become on-line on Zoom gatherings. Even the General Conference, which had been postponed until September of 2021, had been postponed yet again. Several other bishops across the church were retiring in 2021 as well.

I spent the spring preparing for my two final Annual Conferences and transitioning my conference work to the bishops who would take my place. They were Bishop Schol from the Greater New Jersey Annual Conference, who would serve Eastern Pennsylvania, and Bishop Easterling from the Baltimore-Washington Conference who would also serve Peninsula-Delaware. Each of these bishops now would have two conferences.

Retiring felt a little like dying, despite my prayerful discernment. I had grown to love the people and the good ministries that were happening in these conferences. There was a twinge of guilt for deserting the ship before the big General Conference in the future that would decide about The Protocol.

The very soul of the denomination was on trial. We were in a holding pattern of sorts, with no clear plan for what the future of the denomination would look like. In a parallel sense, the United States was also in a state of turmoil over the 2020 election results, racism, climate change, opioid addiction, gun violence escalation, immigrants seeking asylum, and the continued and controversial roll-out of the first COVID vaccinations.

Vaccines were helping to stem the tide of the pandemic in the United States and around the world, and COVID restrictions in the U.S. were being relaxed in many areas. Restaurants were opening again, planes were flying, mask requirements were becoming discretionary. Our churches began opening again for in person worship services and activities. Just about all of them, however, reported a smaller number of people in the pews on Sunday but, since most of them had been operating with virtual options prior to reopening, many had obtained a new constituency of people who wanted to continue to participate in church services from their homes. Church was never going to be the same, and many pastors were exhausted by it all.

"DISAFFILIATIONS OF THE HEART"

Large gatherings were still considered to be unsafe by COVID experts, so my spring sessions of the 2021 Annual Conferences were again conducted by Zoom with ordination and memorial services in-person by invitation only and with live-streaming options. Unlike our fall 2020 meetings, which had limited debate and amendments the new rules of order, this time around we would allow both. I cringed at the potential time crisis that a protracted debate on Zoom might create. As it turned out, to my great relief these options were not used very much. Six months into this electronic way of living had created a more sophisticated clientele of conference participants, both lay and clergy. Most people seemed by this time to be more comfortable with voting electronically, and individual system failures were at a minimum.

Though most of my two Annual Conferences went on without a hitch, it was the Peninsula Delaware Conference that had many disaffiliations and caused me the most personal heartache. There were eleven disaffiliating churches that petitioned to leave, and they were all from the conservative side of the house. Armed with "the bishop won't do church trials" as their rationale, they sought disaffiliation to become independent entities. Homosexuality could be blamed for it, but my overwhelming impression was it was motivated by a political discontent with the winds of change in our country and the fear of change in the hearts of many.

THE EVER-EXPANSIVE SPIRIT OF GOD

One congregation's disaffiliation was prompted by their pastor's speech at a board meeting, warning his church about the upcoming "take-over" by the future Baltimore-Washington Conference's new bishop who the pastor charged promoted progressive political agendas. This pastor insinuated that his church would have to be paying more apportionment dollars to support what he called the "failing liberal churches." These statements were not factual, but this presentation went viral on a video Facebook post, and many additional churches requested to disaffiliate as well.

The eleven disaffiliating churches brought their resolutions to this electronic session of the Peninsula-Delaware Conference. One of them included a particularly mean-spirited addition to their petition that called me out personally for failing to keep my consecration vows as a bishop.

When this resolution was presented, a member of one of our progressive churches gave the following speech:

The authors of this Resolution have a certain tunnel vision which, for all intents and purposes, has actually blinded them from the light and Word of the Gospel of Jesus Christ. The faith that these persons claim is prejudicially biased, intestinally homophobic, and diametrically opposed to the Gospel message of love and salvation in the name of Jesus Christ.

"DISAFFILIATIONS OF THE HEART"

In raising a prophetic voice to those who seek to wallow in misinterpretation of Scripture and the misdirected practice of hatred of those who have been created in the image of God, Bishop Peggy Johnson has followed in the footsteps of prophets of old, who spoke truth to power.

Nothing further was said after that speech. I was forever grateful that someone spoke on my behalf. All the churches that petitioned for disaffiliation in the Peninsula-Delaware Conference were approved at the Annual Conference session. They were required to pay a number of prescribed fees and complete much legal documentation, but they were essentially free of the denomination

I could not leave my position as an active bishop without a deep sense of sadness over it all. I felt a "disaffiliation of the heart" in a sense. Across the denomination in 2021, there were approximately 130 churches disaffiliating and most of them were theologically conservative.

26

"UNMOORED"

The time for my retirement from active ministry drew near in the summer of 2021. There were a series of Zoom farewell events, a good-natured roast, luncheons, and groups visiting my office with gifts and hugs. Everyone was immensely gracious and generous. and it felt much like when I was first elected to the episcopacy back in 2008. Every gift, letter, card, flower, box of chocolates and offering to the Congo Partnership Mission in my honor was as kind as it could be, but I still felt a deep sadness.

Mary, my spouse, shared this parting grief with me. She had officially retired in January of 2021 but continued to serve a church as an interim during the first four months of 2021. When September came around, we would both be without a congregation to serve for the first time since 1978. It was hard to get our heads around this, as active ministry was all we ever knew as a couple.

What got me through was the inward certainty that God was calling me to retire and that it was the right thing to do at this time. Mary could finally be her true self, we would be able to be a part of our grandson's life, and I would be free to engage in some new ministries. Yet leaving these people I had served and loved for thirteen years felt like being in a ship without a tether to the dock, floating out to sea, unmoored and without a rudder.

As we packed, down-sized, and sorted our belongings and books, my beloved spouse loaded up all her male clothing: professional men's' suits, argyle sweaters, wing-tipped shoes, everything, and dropped them off at the Good Will Thrift Store (the same one where she secretly bought female clothing during the beginning of her transition). Mary was going to dress as a woman when we moved to Virginia, in our new home, in our new life. This too felt like unmooring. I had been tethered to the closet life of everyone thinking that my spouse was a man. As uncomfortable as that closet can be, it was safe.

Before we left Pennsylvania, Mary wrote to her mother and siblings and let them know her true gender. Then she flew to Texas, where most of them lived, to help them process this transition announcement in person. The news was not altogether understood by her family, but like the decent, salt-of-the-earth people they are, they asked their questions and let the bonds of love remain unbroken. Some had suspected for a long time that something like this had been going on.

I wrote my last bishop's blog, titled "A Time to Keep and a Time to Cast Away," and sent it to my conference communicators to be sent to everyone on all our lists. I thanked people for their faithfulness, asked for forgiveness for any hurts I may have caused them, and enumerated the many blessings I had received from them that I intended to keep in my heart. I ended the blog with these words:

As I was packing boxes in the attic the other day, I found a box labeled "Election" and in it were various memoirs of the day I became a bishop (July 17, 2008). Among the various letters of congratulations, pictures and programs was a little scrap of notebook paper with a scripture passage on it. I remember writing these words on my first day in the Philadelphia Area on September 1, 2008. The words from Zechariah 7:9-10 were like a mandate from God for what I needed to do as bishop: "This is what the Lord Almighty says: administer true justice, show mercy and compassion to one another, do not oppress the widow or the fatherless, the alien or the poor. In your hearts do not think evil of each other."

I will keep these words from the Bible in my heart and in my future life, and I leave them with you to follow as well. Never cast these words away, but keep them

"UNMOORED"

always; and if you do these things, you will truly be the church that God intends.

~

Our moving day was August 10, 2021, and we traveled six hours south to our residence in a condo community in Carrollton, Virginia. The neighborhood has a good mixture of ages and ethnicities, and many folks stopped by to greet us when we arrived. Our moving dates happened to be during a week-long heat wave, with a daily heat index of 107 degrees. It took three days in all to move with the packing, loading, and delivery. The movers worked early and quickly, and it was a blur of opening boxes, hanging pictures, and arranging all the women's clothing in one closet!

I was still on the clock as the bishop of my area until the first of September, so I kept in touch with the conference superintendents and staff by phone and email for three more weeks. It was a bit of a security blanket to be able to still do something I was used to doing, during a time that was feeling very strange and new in Virginia. When August 31 came and I finally disconnected my business phone and talked to the district superintendents for the last time, I sat in the living room with the lights off and wondered what the future would bring.

THE EVER-EXPANSIVE SPIRIT OF GOD

That first Sunday we were in Virginia, we attended worship at the nearby Ebenezer United Methodist Church, a church we had visited in the past when we were in Virginia on vacation visiting our oldest son. It is a large, colonial-looking church with a sizable congregation. Mary wore a woman's pantsuit, one that I had carefully shopped for before we moved. She wore her hair in a bun and put on earrings and a matching necklace.

The director of the children's ministry was preaching that day and I noticed that she signed some of her words in her sermon as she went along. Just seeing a little American Sign Language was a sign from God for me that we were in the right place, despite how uncomfortable I felt with my spouse in female attire in public for the first time.

As God would have it, my former therapist, the one who counseled me when Mary first came out to me in 2010, contacted me out of the blue on Facebook and told me about a Zoom support group called "Cisters"—a gathering of women who were cisgender females married to men who had either transitioned to female, were in the process of doing so, or were gender fluid. The name of the group was a clever pun. We were all cisgender wives with unique spouses. (*Cisgender* means any person whose gender that was assigned at birth and their inward understanding of the gender match.)

I eagerly joined this gathering one Wednesday evening, and around the Zoom screen were about twenty women of all ages from various parts of the country. The therapist and another colleague in the field facilitated the conversation with questions, and participants could weigh in as they felt led. For my benefit, the therapist asked each woman to give a short summary about her life situation. Some were like me with long marriages and a transition in mid-life. Some had spouses that were just beginning the process, some were married to cross-dressers who would present as either male or female depending on the day. All were out to their wider community and friends, and some had paid a dear price for this, especially the "cisters" who lived in more conservative parts of the country. Those living in a more liberal part of the United States had a distinct advantage of acceptance and accessibility.

When it was my turn, I said that I had recently retired and had previously worked for the church. (I didn't say which one, or my role in the church), and that Mary and I were starting to come out to the world. I expressed my uneasiness attending church for the first time with a female-looking spouse. They all understood. The "cisters" were loving and supportive, and it was so helpful to be with them on their monthly Zoom calls.

The next Sunday we went back to the same church, and this time Mary wore a bright green flowered skirt and we could see the puzzled look on the pastor's face. We made an appointment to meet with the pastor to explain our situation. Rev. Won Lee received us with grace and a non-judgmental attitude. He shared that the congregation, though not liberal, was not strongly conservative either and that likely things would be OK with us participating in the life of the congregation. Mary and I later met with some of the leadership at a "meet and greet" luncheon and experienced this to be true. We continued to attend, mostly at the sparsely attended early service. We did not want to be around a lot of people due to the COVID pandemic, which was beginning its third wave.

One Sunday we visited an old pastor friend from the Baltimore-Washington Conference who had recently been appointed to a new church in Virginia, about an hour away from our home. Rev. Hae Rin Lawson's church was welcoming, and she and her family embraced Mary and I fully. A few weeks later, I joined a United Methodist Women's group for fellowship, volunteered at an area food bank, attended the condo's community association board meetings and met several of our new neighbors. I even connected with a Deaf fellowship group that met at a local mall every month.

As these church and community connections began to happen, my feeling of being unmoored began to subside. I simply had to live one day at a time.

27

"THE REVEAL"

As the weeks wore on, Mary and I continued to widen the circle of people who knew that she was a woman. I contacted the United Methodist bishop of the Virginia Annual Conference where we were living to let her know about the church we were attending in her area. I assured Bishop Sharma Lewis that I would inform her if anything came up that she should know. She thanked me and that was the beginning of the door opening.

Next Mary contacted her bishop, Bishop LaTrelle Easterling, from the Baltimore-Washington Conference, where Mary's clergy membership remained, even while I was serving as the bishop in the Philadelphia Area. Mary sent Bishop Easterling a hard copy "reveal" letter. As soon it was in the mailbox, I texted the bishop and asked that she call me after she read it. This she did, and we talked a long time. The news was a complete surprise to her, but she responded with grace and support. This revelation began to feel like a little taste of freedom and not as dreadful as I had imagined.

~

After that it was important to let the other bishops of the denomination and their spouses know. I informed Bishop John Schol, who was now serving as the episcopal leader of the Eastern Pennsylvania Conference, and he too was supportive. Then I contacted the president of the Council of Bishops, Bishop Cynthia Harvey, and she and the executive committee of the Council approved my plan to first send a coming-out letter to the Northeastern Jurisdiction College of Bishops and then to the entire Council of Bishops.

My heart knew it was time to tell the bishops, but as I was ready to press the send button on this reveal email, I took a deep breath and felt a twinge of apprehension. I felt intensely vulnerable, and there was a part of me that did not want to look different in the eyes of my colleagues. Prayer was a great source of comfort at that time and so was the music of Rachmaninoff.

I played Rachmaninoff's *Vocalise*, that soulful cello solo, repeatedly during these weeks of the reveal. It was the song that had echoed in my mind and heart like a relentless earworm eleven years earlier when Mary first came out to me. I sought it out again for strength to journey through this time as well.

"THE REVEAL"

The bishops who responded to our coming out were generous and kind. They offered friendship and prayers. Many commented on our "profound courage," for our "public witness," and for the "marital love that we shared." Some noted that our eleven years in the closet while I was serving as an active bishop must have been like "walking a tightrope." All promised continued prayers for our journey of ministry, and many sent follow-up cards and letters. Some of the bishops' spouses who knew Mary well also wrote personal notes to her. There were about forty responses in all, but there was no response from the majority of the United Methodist bishops, all of whom were my colleagues.

Because Mary was to take part in the virtual retirement celebration for the Baltimore-Washington Annual Conference session in November, it seemed wise to have them publish a story about this transition ahead of time. Her appearing as Mary at this event, without any prior understanding of her transgender reality would have been an odd, or perhaps even a disruptive moment at this celebration. With the bishop's support, the editor of the church's national paper, Melissa Lauber, interviewed Mary and I and penned a sensitive and informative article for the Baltimore-Washington Conference weekly newsletter.

The article included additional informational website links, and it could not have been handled with more grace and transparency. It was due to be published on Monday, October 11, 2021, which just happened to be National Coming Out Day. It was not our intent to choose that day. But likely people thought we chose this date intentionally. I think perhaps God planned it that way.

The week before the publication of the story, both extended cabinets in the Eastern Pennsylvania and Peninsula-Delaware Conferences were made aware of this forthcoming announcement. I received many emails, cards, and gifts from people in response. I contacted the chair of the Northeastern Jurisdictional Committee on Episcopacy, Bonnie Marden, and let her know so she could be in touch with this committee before it hit the media. She held a Zoom meeting with the committee one evening, and I responded to their questions.

I also connected with the president of the United Methodist Reconciling Ministry Network (RMN) around this same time. This is the official caucus of the church that advocates for LGBTQIA inclusion. Jan Lawrence, the president was supportive and interested in our future involvement with the transgender committee of RMN known as UMATI (United Methodist Alliance for Transgender Inclusion).

My conversations with RMN included the unfinished business of the church trial for the Eastern Pennsylvania Conference pastor back in 2013. Though not the charging party, I was the bishop who sent Rev. Schaefer to trial, and some in RMN were still unsettled with me because of my role in this ordeal. I produced a statement and video

"THE REVEAL"

apology which was posted on the RMN website, which may or may not have been helpful. Understandably, the pain of a church trial is not easily dismissed, if ever.

The weekend before the publication date of the Baltimore-Washington Conference's article, I was on the phone making calls to personal friends, extended family, and local church leaders where we had previously served. I wanted to be sure they got the word from me before they read about it in the news or heard about it second-hand. Making these calls was exhausting, and some asked innocent but insensitive questions that were hard to answer. I felt that anxious sense of no turning back in my heart each time I made a call. Mary and I did not sleep well on the night of October 10, 2021, and Rachmaninoff played in my head relentlessly.

Early the next morning, the article appeared on the internet as promised and immediately my phone started ringing and my email in-box was filled with literally hundreds of responses. Every one of them was positive, loving, and supportive. For weeks after that, handwritten notes and greeting cards filled our mailbox as if it was Christmas. Those who disagreed or were puzzled kept silent for the most part. A few snarky posts appeared on Facebook, a few folks sent painful letters, and a derogatory blog could be found on a conservative organization's website, but we were surprised there was not more overt negativity.

Some in the United Methodist transgender community who were already out and still actively serving felt that we should have come out sooner and not waited until retirement, when it was safe. I could understand that sentiment, but few people know the extent of the pressures of being an episcopal leader. We answered each email of concern with grace, knowing that the LGBTQIA community is as diverse and nuanced in their opinions as any other group of people.

We were having window blinds installed in our home on that day. The installation team was bustling around the house putting up these adjustable shades with ladders and electric screw drivers. I told them to leave the upper blinds open as we needed sunshine to fill the house. Revealing Mary's true gender identity to the world that day was like shining rays of light into that closet of darkness we had endured for so long.

The next day the National United Methodist News Service picked up the story and it literally went around the world. Closet no more! Several weeks later the article was reprinted in the *Christian Century Magazine*. We heard from total strangers who are transgender or gender non-conforming, thanking us for making this a visible and human issue. Some shared that they too were in a cisgender/transgender marriage and understood our situation quite well. A new window for ministry had opened. This was what I wanted more than anything else to come from our reveal.

In the weeks and months that followed we met with several cisgender/transgender couples on Zoom calls. We have been invited to speak at various classes, PFLAG groups, Sunday School classes, Reconciling Ministry Network committees, and churches to explain the reality of gender identity as a spectrum—not a fixed binary.

One of our greatest joys was to participate together in a worship service at the historic Dumbarton United Methodist Church in Washington, DC. This congregation was celebrating thirty-five years of being welcoming and affirming, a "Reconciling" congregation. Early in their journey of inclusive ministry, they penned a landmark document explaining about the transgender community. It was the first of its kind in the United Methodist constellation.

Mary preached that day at Dumbarton and told her life's story. She reminded the congregants to believe people if they come out to them as transgender, as it could literally save their life. I presided at the communion table (using American Sign Language) at this service along with the pastor, Rev. Rachel Cornwell. She and her husband have a trans child and are active in the movement of educating and encouraging support for young trans people. (Rachel recently published a very important book

THE EVER-EXPANSIVE SPIRIT OF GOD

titled *Daring Adventures: Helping Gender-Diverse Kids and Their Families Thrive.*)

For the first time ever, I wore a rainbow-colored stole as I blessed the bread and the cup. At the close of the service, the congregation stood in a circle in the sanctuary and sang a contemporary hymn, *Draw the Circle Wide*, and it felt as if those words had come to fruition for me for the very first time.

We continue to answer emails from people across the country seeking more information. When Christmas 2021 rolled around, we signed our Christmas cards Peggy and Mary for the first time and it was like the birth of a new reality for both of us. There were no more secrets, no more double life.

There is no greater gift that anyone can get than the gift of recognition and affirmation for who they know themselves to be in this world. I end this book with a reminder that this gift is costly, but it is also precious. We as human beings can make peace in this world by offering this gift of acceptance and grace to one another. That includes acceptance for people who are Deaf; people with disabilities; people who are lesbian, gay, bisexual, transgender, queer, intersex, agender, asexual, non-binary, two-spirit; people of color; people struggling for immigration rights; women who are oppressed; and people with whom we disagree. Only with love can we overcome the obstacles that keep us waging war against one another. God's Spirit continues to expand to include more and more people in this circle of love.

The journey of the United Methodist Church and its official stance on homosexuality has yet to be lived out at a session of General Conference now slated for the spring of 2024. However, General Conference is not the place where the real work is accomplished. We do it locally, with the humans we encounter daily. That is where we can make peace and practice tolerance and grace, where there is hope for all who are left out.

ADVANCE PRAISE FOR
The Ever-Expansive Spirit of God

In her pastoral ministry with the Deaf communities, Peggy Johnson learned to hear with her heart; in her role as a presiding bishop, she encountered others on the edges who were equally tenacious in their struggles to live freely— including her own spouse. Through it all, her faith enabled her to count on the promise of what she calls "the ever-expanding Spirit of God," a Spirit that always equips the called and always enables new life. — Bishop Susan M. Morrison, United Methodist Church

In this painfully honest first-hand account of some of the biggest headlines in United Methodist history over the last twenty years, Bishop Peggy Johnson juxtaposes her commitments to ministry, family, and a deeply divided church. There are no easy answers here, but there is real testimony about the process of trying to stay in relationship through discord and difference. — Mx. Chris Paige, M.Div., author, *Other-Wise Christian: A Guidebook for Transgender Liberation*

This needed and timely memoir testifies to the fact and faith that not only is there *Hope for All Who Feel Left Out* but, in fact, the "Left Out" among us possess salvific grace we desperately need in these times. From the inquiring beginning to the stories of tumultuous events in the middle to the transformative hope-filled journey at the end, these six words in the final chapter, "coming out will save your lives," ring an eternal and intersectional song of salvation for us all!
—Bishop Alfred Johnson, United Methodist Church